The Angels Made Me Do It

Pat Dolan

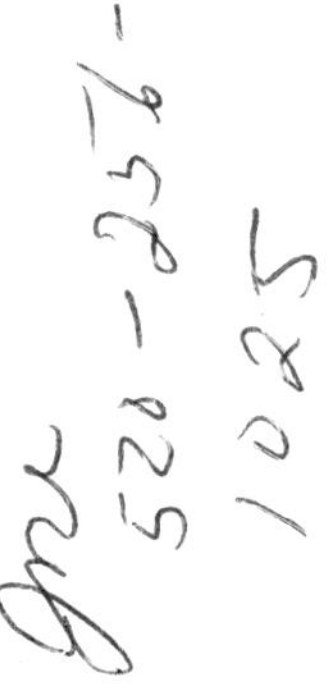

Drawings and Cover Art by Pat Dolan

Dedicated to my granddaughter Ava,
who already knows how to speak her truth.

Author Biography

I wear many hats; artist, writer, healer, teacher/mentor, traveler, seeker, and aspiring stand-up comedian. I live in Oracle, Arizona, with my golden doodle Parker, a therapy dog, Feliz, a tuxedo cat who is always alpha, and 11 goldfish, more or less, depending on how hungry the local raccoons are.

Thank You

To my Editor, Ellen Steiber, who transformed my ramblings into a book, Imo Baird's dynamic design that made this book come to life, and my buddies Carol Ostrander and Erica Swadley, who corrected my cavalier approach to punctuation and spelling. I also want to thank my cheerleader friends who believed in me and encouraged me all along the way. Thanks to Sylvia Minot, my zoom writing companion, champion, and movement mentor. Gratitude to my family, who see me and are amused and interested in my take on the spirit world. No more rolled eyes when I talk about my chats with the dead and the angels. Thanks to the White Table mediums; Annemarie, Susan, Lucinda, Ellen, Erica, Carol, Sophia, and Dawn. You are compassionate women who radiate love. I am blessed to be in your company. Thank you to the spirit world, including my power animals and teachers. And finally, the Angels who Made Me Do It. You guys are so full of love and laughter. What's next, or should I even ask?

ISBN 978-0-9985237-2-9
Published by Brigid's Well
www.patdolan.net
Copyright © 2022 by Pat Dolan

Contents

Illustrations

Angel of Liberty

1 Kicking the bucket, shuffling off these mortal coils—then what happens?

I have been pondering what happens when you die since I was eight years old and began attending weekly catechism classes at Saint Francis Xavier Catholic Church in Wilmette, Illinois.

Sister Mary Margaret, our teacher, felt that it was her job to teach the nuances of sin, especially the categories of mortal sin. According to Sister Mary Margaret, mortal sin, including murder and adultery, was a ticket straight to hell. Now I was a little perplexed by adultery. She mentioned something about coveting your neighbor's wife, and I didn't have a clue what coveting meant.

Rather than embarrassing myself, I decided to go home and ask my fallen-away Irish Catholic dad to explain adultery to me. I went upstairs and found my dad reading, and I asked him to please explain adultery to me as I was a bit confused.With a bit of a twinkle in his eye, he announced that it was one of the seven deadly sins, and he proceeded to explain gluttony, like when you eat too much food at Thanksgiving. Okay. I nodded. Got it.

The following Saturday, I marched into the confessional and said to the priest, "Bless me, Father, for I have sinned. I was mean to my brother and committed adultery once." I think I heard the priest mumble "Jesus" under his breath. I was thinking of the time I ate all those Oreo cookies over at Wendy's house. I said, "Yeah, I just couldn't help myself." Then I heard the priest exclaimed, "*Jesus, Mary and Joseph!*" a lot in the same tone my father would use when things were about to hit the fan. He then mumbled something like, "Ten 'Our Fathers' and ten 'Hail Marys,'" and I left the confessional, relieved that I no longer had a mortal sin on my soul.

Mortal sins give you a direct ticket to hell forever—terrible news—but I didn't think I would rack up a bunch of mortal sins. I was a kid, sure I was going to heaven where there were fluffy heaven clouds, beautiful music, and lots of smiling angels. However, it soon became clear to me that the only way I would get to heaven was if I'd gone to Confession, then gone to Mass and received Communion, and then on my way across the street to catechism class I was hit by a bus. My thinking was that I would have a completely white soul at that moment in time. The problem was that my white soul would not last because as soon as I got home, I would be mean to my brother or not do something my mother wanted me to and then all of a sudden, I was having a collection of sins that were going to impede my ascent to heaven.

All that was left for me and my afterlife was Purgatory, a rather grim Catholic invention. Sister Mary Margaret described it as a slightly milder version of hell. Lots of flames but the good news was that eventually you got to leave Purgatory and go up to heaven. The rub was that no one knew how long your stay in Purgatory would be, though I did my best to get an answer from Sister Mary Margaret—"Are we talking a hundred days? A thousand days? A *million* days?" The number of days I was likely destined to spend in Purgatory was a deep concern of mine. Maybe I needed to stop overeating the Oreo cookies. I soon concluded that dying and the afterlife were nothing but bad news if you were a Catholic. I was doomed.

Years later, after attending a Catholic women's college, I decided to hand in my Catholic card and search for a more upbeat take on the afterlife. In studying my pagan druidic roots, I decided to embrace *Tir na nog*, the Celtic otherworld where you go after you die to feast, laugh, and dance.

Resting Angel

2 Why "*The Angels Made Me Do It*"?

This book started out to describe my experiences talking to the dead via a Brazilian White Table. The purpose of the White Table is to assist the dead in crossing into the Light. A group of people acting as mediums sit together in meditation and are open to receiving the spirits of the dead and speaking for them. Before we begin each White Table session, we call in the spirits of the five Archangels—Archangel Michael, Archangel Gabriel, Archangel Raphael, Archangel Uriel, and Archangel Metatron—to create a dome of protection while we do our work in the land of the dead. Little did I know that this would be the beginning of my rather close relationship with the world of angels.

However, the book's subject matter began to shift during the 2020 Covid pandemic when we could no longer meet in person, and our White Table sessions became virtual. Once a month, at 4 p.m., we would sit down in our separate homes and meditate. We would connect to the energy of our virtual White Table with the intention to be available to assist the deceased and receive messages from the spirits.

What happened in our White Table sessions shifted—from psychopomp work, i.e., guiding souls into the Light, to mainly receiving messages from the spirits. For example, we received messages about how to cope with Covid, the fears, the despair and isolation; how beauty was still available to us and how singing was healing. We'd already learned that the angels and the dead love music so we always played soothing music during White Table.

While writing the book, a group of spirits—later, I discovered that the spirits were actually the Five Archangels, who at first kept me in the dark about their identity. Sly ones those angels, they requested that I become their scribe.

Demanded might be a better choice of words. I mean no disrespect, but they can sometimes be pushy despite all their love and light. I'm just saying.

The dialogues I had with the spirits became another aspect to the book. Maybe I was not exactly trying to weasel my way out of this job, but I wanted to get some clarification. When dealing with the spirit world, if you ask them to help you in whatever domain it might be, and they then ask something of you, you can't exactly say, "Oh, gosh, I don't know. I don't want to. I have to organize my sock drawer."

So I decided to just go along with the angels' program. Okay, and maybe to whine a bit. Part of our conversation was about me not feeling qualified for the job. They soon convinced me I was the right person and could do it. Then the Archangels tapped into my skills as a visual artist. Not only did they want me to be their scribe, but they wanted me to paint "their portraits and portraits of their Angel friends." Painting the angels was an easy request for me and great fun.

When I started painting angels, I thought about how they had traditionally been portrayed as sweet or sentimental. I wanted to paint them with juice, and I wanted them to be an inspiration to the viewer. In the fall of 2021, I decided to paint an angel a day for November. Once I started, I couldn't stop painting angels. Headlines affected what angels I painted. For example, I painted an *angel defending Democracy and the people of Ukraine.*I donated the proceeds from the giclee prints of Ukraine angels to help the Ukraine refugees. When I discovered I was to become a grandmother, I painted an angel dancing through the sky, naming her *I believe in miracles.* The paintings grew looser and more anecdotal. After a group of marauding raccoons emptied my koi pond of fish and water, I painted the guardian angel of the goldfish. Each day, I looked forward to painting these angels. They made me laugh. I seemed to be gripped by the idea of creating images of angels that highlighted their personalities. Some angels expressed hope, some frustration, and many love and compassion.

Painting angels gave me an excuse to impulse buy new art supplies. I needed gold paint and pens, new Gouache watercolors in opera pink, brilliant purple, turquoise, ultramarine blue, and lots of cadmium yellows. One angel seemed to require a set of googly eyes.

After I painted about forty of these divine beings, the angels more or less pushed themselves into this book. They made it clear that they were part of it—and they had meant to be part of it from the very start. Ergo, these angel illustrations.

Recently, during a virtual White Table session, they told me the following:

The Archangels: *We are so enjoying your paintings of us. They are so full of life. Ha ha, since we were never alive . . . well, maybe a few of us, were once alive. Yes, Ellen was spot on. Lilith was a kickass angel and the men demoted her.*Yes, reclaim her and her power, and in reclaiming her, you shall reclaim your power.*

The White Table work must go out into the world, and we will help you. One goal of the White Table is to help lost souls cross over. Another goal is to bring messages from the dead to their loved ones. Then the messages and teachings from the spirit world come through. All of these goals are equally important.

We angels are very user-friendly. Who doesn't like a nice chat with an angel? Even if you're an atheist. We are non-denominational, outside the church or religions. No pun intended.

We angels are a gateway to the spirit world. Think of us as the equivalent of Walmart greeters. We greet folks and invite them to step into the world of spirit. This realm is one of imagination and play. Hanging out with us is fun.

Angel Defending Democracy

3 How I became so gripped about talking to our dead

In 1961 when my father died, I was fourteen and no one talked about dead parents. Nor did my mother think that my brother, sister, and I were also grieving his loss. So, I took all my grief, stuffed it down, and never spoke of my father's life or death to anyone for ten years. I became so depressed that I finally went to a psychiatrist. I think he acknowledged the profound loss of my father, but I left not having a clue how to grieve.

My sister Pam was killed in a car crash when I was thirty-one. Again her loss was devastating; again, I had no clue how to deal with my grief. I remember spending many hours talking to Charles, my best friend (and a year later, my husband), about Pam's death. Why her? She was twenty-five and living in Chicago, working for a major advertising company.

After many months, I finally got to a place where I realized that there was no explanation or reason for the death of a loved one, especially one so young. Somehow that gave me some peace.

However, in 1991 when Charles, my husband, art partner, father of our son, best friend and lover, died, I was gobsmacked. With the help of friends, I made it through the funeral.

Our son Patrick was six, and I didn't want him to go through what I did when my father died. I contacted Children to Children, a non-profit organization that aims to support grieving children. Every month, Patrick and I would drive to Tucson to attend the grief groups at Children to Children. Patrick played, drew, and ran outside in his group. We sat in a circle in the adult group and talked, cried, and whispered our losses.

I mistakenly thought that if one grief group helped, two grief groups would hasten the healing and remove the grey veil of grief that enveloped me. I joined a second grief group at Shanti, which supports people living with a terminal illness. By 1992 the terminal illness was AIDS. I joined the grief group led by Fritz, who was caring, compassionate, wise, and very funny. He shared a lot about what his journey was after his partner died. We all cried together and laughed together. Each of us felt like we had found a place where we belonged that was safe and nurturing.

Six months later, Fritz drew me aside and asked me to lead the grief group. I was stunned. He told me that he could no longer lead the group as he was HIV+ and needed to focus on living not dying. I was devastated to learn that he was sick. "Not him," I said to myself.

Izzie as an Angel Now

4 Everything you never wanted to know about grief

So I began to lead grief groups in the middle of my own grieving.In one session, we talked about the crazy things we all did to connect with our deceased loved ones. My friend Philippe said he would turn over the photo of his partner John every night, hoping that John would visit him in the night and turn the photo up as a sign. Each morning the photo remained facedown. About four months after Charles died, I needed to buy new tires. At the tire store, I looked at the various tires from cheap to Michelin, which were very expensive. Charles liked to buy cheap tires at Sears.I thought: *If I buy the expensive tires, it will put him over the edge and he'll come back to keep me from these extravagant purchases.* Part of my mind knew that he was dead. I saw him die and I buried him. But it was worth a try in some other part of my mind. Six hundred dollars later Charles did not appear.

Patrick and I continued to attend the programs Children to Children until Patrick said, "Enough, Mom."

In 1999 I decided to become a certified grief counselor through the Association of Death Education and Counseling (ADEC). I wanted to learn about grief—my own and how to support others in their grieving process. In preparation to take an exam to become certified as a grief counselor through ADEC, I took a great death and dying class with Dr. Robert Wrenn at the University of Arizona. He covered everything one needed to know about grief with humor and compassion. In his class I read J. William Worden's book, *Grief Counseling and Grief Therapy*, in which he identifies the Four Tasks of Mourning:

1. To accept the reality of the loss
2. To work through the pain of grief
3. To adjust to an environment in which the deceased is missing
4. To find an enduring connection with our dearly departed.

Since Charles' death, I'd been working on the first three. But Task 4? That was another story.

5 Beyond the grave—hey, are they all okay?

I was intrigued by Task 4: finding and keeping an enduring connection with our dead. For me that meant recreating the relationship with Charles now that I could no longer sit and have a chat with him or feel his arms wrapped around me. It was not at all clear how to do that. In my grief process, I found adjusting to an environment where the deceased was missing was very difficult. It took me many months of wandering around in my grief, attending grief groups, and writing letters to Charles, before I could begin to imagine my life without him. And that was only part of the problem. I wanted to contact Charles. I just needed to know that he was okay.

The one time, forty years ago, that I'd gone to a psychic was because I wanted to know that my deceased family members were okay—my dad, my sister Pam, and my grandmother Nan. The psychic contacted them and assured me that they were fine. I remember her telling me that Nan was dancing through the afterlife and was very happy. So I figured this was true for Charles—that he was okay—but I wanted more. I wanted to talk with him.

At an ADEC (Association for Death Educators and Counselors) conference, I walked into a room for a breakout session about communicating with our deceased loved ones. There were thirty mothers in the room and every one of them had visited a psychic to find out if their children who had died were okay. As a result of this experience I realized I had to find a way to communicate with the dead to help myself and others who were grieving. It seemed that was a missing piece in the grief journey.

In 1992, I discovered Michael Harner's trainings in cross-cultural shamanism. Michael adapted a way for people to get into an altered state of consciousness, or non-ordinary reality, through the repetitious beat of a drum. We were taught how to contact our spirit guides and travel through non-ordinary reality.

In a shamanic journey one listens to a recording of a repetitious drumbeat or rattle which changes the brain waves and puts one into a light trance. It's referred to as a journey, as being in that trance state allows you to travel to other worlds. When I learned this technique of connecting with my helping spirits, I liked it because it was so simple. You listen to simple, repetitive drumming. (At the time I used tapes, but now you can buy or download a CD.) Then you close your eyes and imagine going into an opening in the earth. There you meet up with your power animal or helping spirit and ask them your question. They answer you directly, by taking you on a trip or through metaphors. It sometimes is a bit like interpreting a dream, only more accessible. You can always ask for a clarification or to be given another symbol or image that makes more sense to you.

I continued studying with Michael Harner, completing The Foundation for Shamanic Studies' Three-Year Program of Advanced Initiations in Shamanism and Shamanic Healing. I was learning how to connect with the spirit realm in all these classes. With practice in journeying my relationships with my spirit guides and power animals became deeper. I no longer felt alone.

Later, I trained with Sandra Ingerman in Soul Retrieval, Extraction and Death and Dying. In these techniques called psychopomp work, we learned to help souls cross over to the Light. The basis of this work is the assumption that after death, all souls want to go the Light.That's our true home—what we came from and must return to.But sometimes souls get stuck in our world because they don't feel worthy to move on, want to stay to help a loved one, or are frightened. So the shamanic practitioner goes on a journey to them and assists them in crossing into the Light.

Before my mother died, she asked me to see if I could contact her after her death. When I first journeyed to my mom after she died, I found her smoking Salem Lights and drinking scotch. It seemed she was not quite ready to cross over and I was not interested in hanging out with her in the Land of the Dead as she drank scotch.Later when I visited her again, she had crossed into the Light.

Shamanic journeying has been part of my spiritual practice for the past thirty years and my contact with souls who had passed over was teaching me that most of them were okay—and that I could help some of the ones who weren't.and Mother Earth.

6 Through the pearly gates . . . oops, where are those gates?

In my shamanic training we did various initiations. In one initiation, we had to guarantee that we would return from our journey back into ordinary reality. This request was unusual. They'd never asked us for a promise like this before. *Of course, I'll come back,* I thought. *I have a son to raise, a house, clients.* It never occurred to me that I wouldn't come back.

In this initiation, we journeyed to the moment after our death. We couldn't see our death, just the moment when we were dead. That journey was profound. As if I was traveling through the Milky Way, I traveled to a land of light. No body, no personality, no ego. I *was* light. I then understood why I had to promise to return. It was so lovely, surrounded by so much love, that it made me just want to stay there. Afterward I was no longer afraid of death.

In the late 2000s when I was in my sixties, I traveled to the Ecuadorian rainforest where I did ayahuasca ceremonies with Achuar shamans. These ayahuasca visions not only deepened my connection with the spirits of nature and Mother Earth, but I had similar experiences of what happens after you die. I was shown the river of light where souls join after they die. I was told to tell people about this, though it was not my time to join the river of light.So no pearly gates, but I was okay with that.The river of light was so much better. And somehow that image felt real.When I painted a large 5'x3' painting of the river of light with a jaguar stepping into it, the image became even more real to me.

7 Okay this is really wild, I can channel the dead?

My hands are resting on the white tablecloth of a long table. Next to me and across from me are twenty other students of Michael Harner's three-year program in Advanced Shamanism and Shamanic Healing. Along another table sits the Sauer family, the mother and her son Carlos, and her daughter Aparecida from Sao Paulo, Brazil. Michael has invited the Sauer family to teach us de-possession.

De-possession involves contacting spirits of deceased human beings who have remained on the earth, rather than moving on. Sometimes those spirits attach themselves to family members or a place where they died. The Sauer family were all trained in the Spiritism tradition.

Spiritism was introduced in Brazil at the end of the nineteenth century. Today, Brazil is the most Spiritist country in the world. With over 3.8 million believers, Spiritism is the third largest religious group after Catholics and evangelicals. Spiritism taught people how to be mediums. The spirits of the dead would come through the medium and the medium would then speak for them. The afterlife is seen by Spiritism not as a static place but as a place where spirits continue to evolve.

Spiritism and Spiritualism are often used interchangeably, with the most notable difference being that Spiritists believe in reincarnation while not all Spiritualists do. Both Spiritists and Spiritualists believe disembodied spirits can communicate and carry-on relationships with incarnate human beings.

The room was very still. The mediums offered a few prayers of protection and gratitude. Then we invited the spirits to come. They knew the drill about talking through the mediums sitting around the table covered with a white tablecloth. All the mediums wore white, making it easier for the spirits to come through us. The idea was to create a calm space without distractions. The music we played during the White Table sessions also soothed the spirit and made the room feel very quiet and peaceful. The intention was healing, hearing the stories of the spirits and then, with love, assisting them in moving into the Light and leaving the earth plane.

At that point I had no idea if I could be a medium. The only time I'd had contact with my dead dad, sister Pam, and Grandmother Nan, I went to a psychic.My visit to a psychic was years ago when my son was six months old. She told me that my dad was healing, my sister too, and Nan was dancing and happy. I found the information about my dead comforting, and I just needed to know that they were okay wherever they were out in the cosmos.

One of the mediums would slowly begin to speak as a spirit came through. Sometimes the person asking for help wanted to know where their dead loved ones were or if they had any messages for the living. Sometimes the living needed to make peace with their dead.

The Sauer family, each one taking turns acting as the interviewer, would start to engage the spirit gently by asking them questions: their name, the circumstances of their death, and what they needed to leave the earth plane and go to the Light.

The container of the White Table consists of the prayers, the absolute stillness, and the focused intention to be of service and assist souls lost or stuck. The group energy all supported the one doing the medium's work.

Several years later, around 2000, Carlos Sauer and his sister Aparecida offered another workshop on White Table work, and my friends Erica and Lucinda joined me.

I realized then that I wanted to continue to do White Table work, but it's not something that can be done alone. I needed a group.

Archangel Gabriel

8 Hey, do you want to come over to my house and talk to the dead?

Before my studies in shamanism, I used to think I had a subconscious that was maybe an inch deep. I didn't do tarot, didn't have any imaginary friends, and I didn't see dead people. Thank God.

I didn't think being a medium was anything I could do, yet I discovered I could. The deal with White Table is that it's a group, and you don't do it alone, and I liked the community aspect. At the time I thought White Table originated in Brazil, but it goes back to Allen Kardec (born Hippolyte Leon Denizard Rivail (1804-1864)) with his book *The Spirits' Book,* which he wrote in Paris in 1804. He was a French educator who studied people talking to the dead in seances.In *The Spirits' Book,* Alan Kardec wrote about his experiences observing mediums contacting the deceased. As a scientist and an educator, he was skeptical at first. Over time, he began to trust the mediums, their information, and how they communicated with the dead.

Spiritism went from Europe to New York and later Brazil. Brazil was very open to it because of their spiritual traditions of Catholicism, Candomblé, Umbanda. (European, African, Indigenous.

I realized that I wanted to continue to do White Table work. Since White Table needs community, I asked some friends to join me.

Nine of us now gather together to conduct White Table sessions. The spirits like to know when we meet, and they like regularity, so we meet on the first Sunday of every month. The relationships we have with each other are so dear, supportive, and loving. That is quite remarkable to me. Each of us brings different gifts to the table. Erica is another artist, shamanic practitioner, and healer who works with crystals and Jin Shin Jyutsu. Lucinda is a gemologist and an herbalist who works with plant medicines and tinctures. Susan does Jin Shin Jyutsu and is a practiced Vipassana meditator. Ellen is a writer and editor. Carol is a dowser and uses healing touch with animals. Sophia does somatic work with clients as well as family counseling. Annemarie is a writer and a life coach. Dawn is a master Reiki practitioner and a gardener.

There is so much energy with the nine of us sitting around the White Table. Everybody makes a considerable contribution by being there, no matter what spirits or information they receive. Each person brings their form of subtle energies to the White Table.

After we gather and ready ourselves for the ceremony, we go into the room where I've prepared a table with a white tablecloth, candles, and water from

Brigid's well and Agua Florida to purify our energy. We invite in our spirit guides and the Archangels for protection. Then we are in sacred space, protected by our power animals, spirit teachers, and many angels.

When we started doing White Table at my house, I didn't have a lot of confidence that spirits would come through me. As we sat around the White Table with our hands on the table you could feel the energy moving around the table and the sense that we were surrounded by spirits, our familiars, and the five Archangels.During White Table sessions, I would sense that a spirit wanted to come through me. It felt like someone was fidgeting next to me, trying to get my attention. Then a part of me would think, *I don't know if this is real. Maybe I'm making it all up* and *I'm too anxious to have a spirit come through me.* But the voice would become more persistent, more intense.

Finally, I would feel the spirit was now inside me, and I would speak for them. Sometimes in an accent. The more we've done it, the more I trust this process. I no longer get the chatter that I'm making it up. When we do this work, we feel protected by the Archangels, the ancestors, light and love, the great Goddess, and the Divine.

When my grandmother Velma—or Nan, as we called her—came through, it was fun. She always said that she was born with a caul and therefore was very psychic, intuitively knowing when someone had died. We used to read the horoscope together. But she lived in a time where none of that was acknowledged or valued.

Velma always "saw" me. We were kindred spirits. She brought me pretty party dresses, encouraged me to dance, and told me I might become a ballerina someday. I loved playing with Nan and her brightly colored costume jewelry, reading horoscopes, and eating grilled cheese sandwiches with dill pickles dipped in sugar.

Nan died in 1975. After all these years, I wondered if my grandmother needed help crossing over. But Velma was already in the Light. She had come to tell me that she was very excited that we were doing this work and congratulated us all. She was funny. She thought the music could be livelier, not so somber—that this was more a party, a celebration, not a funeral. We could all lighten up a bit.

Lucinda asked her if she could organize the souls who wanted help. Nan said, "This is not like a bakery, and I will not give everybody a number. This is not my job. I just came through to say this is all great and now I will go dance." It was fun, and I was so happy to know that she was in such great shape.

The tone of the ceremony changed and became more serious. We took turns being the interviewers, sometimes several of us interviewing the same spirit.

We intend to be open for spirits to come through us or to get messages from the deceased at the White Table. One of the things we have realized is that in doing White Table we have become very available to the spirits, and the spirits are open to us. We have been told that we have ancestors who did this kind of mediumship work before.

When I sit at the White Table I go into a trance. Me with my Pat personality disappears and I become an open channel. I feel a nudge or a few words inside my head. As soon as I stop doubting and start trusting, I begin to speak. I have no idea who or what I am saying, I just start talking.

We all are mediums, letting the spirits come through us, and we take turns being the Interviewer. There is so much love and compassion in the room. No one is judged or blamed. It's all about love. Each soul who comes through us is loved and was loved in their lives. White Table helps them reach the Light by connecting them with that love.Unlike the Catholic view of the afterlife that I grew up with, White Table has no blame, just love on the other side for souls. No matter how they lived their life. The whole idea is to help that soul go to the Light, and there is always someone who loves them to welcome them to the Light. If not a person, then a dog or mouse or beloved pet. There's no punishment, and there's no "sin." Everybody gets to go to the Light. To experience that love for all souls over and over again made it real to me.

Sometimes the souls who come through are irreverent, funny, shocked, or surprised, but they're always relieved that they can move on. People who die suddenly often get stuck in our realm because they don't realize they're dead. People who have committed suicide, usually stay. They might feel guilty about how they lived their lives and think they don't deserve to be free from their suffering. Guilt will keep them trapped.

I once felt a nun come through me who was very sad, full of guilt. She was a sister who was a teacher at Our Lady of Angels School in Chicago. She and some young students died in the fire that killed 95 in 1958. She stayed in the classroom with the children as the fire trapped them, praying for God to save them. Some children jumped out the window; many died. In White Table, Sister Mary's spirit came through. She felt it was her fault that they died. Yet, when we asked her, she could see the Light. She waited for the children to cross over and then followed them to the Light.

A cowboy came through me. I saw him lying on the desert floor—he must have fallen from his horse. He wasn't sure what had happened or where he was. I asked him whom he loved. He said he loved his horse Lucky, "best damn horse there ever was." He looked up, saw the Light and his horse. He ran up to his horse, grabbed his mane, and rode Lucky into the Light.

One afternoon we were in ceremony and as I sat at the table with my friends, resting my hands on the linen cloth, I realized that White Table could be reassuring for others whose loved ones had died, as it was reassuring for me. It all seems comforting. My mother has come through, as has my sister Pam, and Charles enjoys popping in now and again. I've watched our other White Table mediums connect with their fathers, mothers, and grandmothers.

For all of us, these experiences have been interesting and consoling, helping us deal with loss and sometimes unraveling earthly struggles.

Also, people can connect to their deceased loved ones in many ways. One way might be that the departed come to visit them in their dreams. If someone is dead and comes into your dreams, you could ask them in your dream, "Do you have a message for me?" Or sometimes, you might just experience their presence. I remember one time after Charles died, I had just taken a nice hot bath and was lying on the couch very relaxed with my hand stretched out. I sensed that Charles was there holding my hand; it was so sweet and comforting. Until my logical brain caught up with me. *Wait a minute,* I thought. *Like, don't I know he's been dead for the last five years?* Then I opened my eyes and he was gone. But that moment of experiencing him holding my hand was quite lovely.

Many people have these experiences, but we don't want people to think we're crazy so we don't speak about it. But then people don't realize that these are very normal experiences. After I shuffle off these mortal coils, I'd like to think that I could, you know, connect to my family and friends. I guess they'd have to want it because the deal is, you gotta be open to the spirits of your dead. They have to work a little bit to shapeshift into how they used to be so we can recognize them. So, needless to say, they're pretty sensitive to who's open to connect with them. They won't do it if you're not open. I guess that's the good news. You don't have to worry that your deceased loved ones are gonna lurk around your dream world or you know, pop in and present themselves at the foot of your bed every night. But if you're open to it and it doesn't freak you out, I think it is a lovely experience. You could just put it out there in a prayer or say, "I would like to connect with you" and see what happens.

In my experiences with White Table Work:

- Love is the healing elixir. Everyone has someone they loved in their life, even if it was their horse or their dog. It's that love that draws the soul to the Light and frees us from being stuck here in the middle world.
- Forgiveness. There is no blame, no making wrong, just compassion.
- Some souls don't want to cross over, because they think they need to stay for their loved ones and help them. In White Table, they learn that they can help their loved ones once they cross over.
- Once deceased, souls initially maintain parts of their personality—funny, impatient, gentle, sweet, gruff. This is also true of souls who have been in Light for years. They come through with parts of their character very much intact so that we recognize them easily.
- Eventually, souls choose love and the Light over staying here.

Archangel Michael Defending Mother Earth

9 So what's up with all these angel paintings?

I don't remember the nuns in Sunday catechism class talking much about angels. However, in their teaching about venal and mortal sin, they mentioned the Holy Ghost who was often disguised as a white bird. He saw everything I did, including not doing what my mother told me to do or even the occasional impure thought. I would have been comforted with the thought of a guardian angel watching over me instead of this spying Holy Ghost. Maybe I didn't have one or at least she was off the job the day I fell off my baby blue 20″ bike and broke my leg. The upside was that I was the hit of my third-grade class because of my crutches.

Later in my forties when I discovered Michael Harner's Foundation for Shamanic Studies I learned that I had power animals who protected me and guided me.

My connection to angels came later in my life after many experiences with spirit animals and teachers in non-ordinary reality.

I remember one afternoon before we had started to hold White Table ceremonies, a friend of mine brought me to meet her friend, an older artist. When we walked in the artist was busy tidying up her living room, placing a white candle, a white rose, and an envelope on her coffee table. She cheerfully explained that she was preparing for a visit with the five Archangels that evening. This piqued my interest. I didn't think much about angels and surely never considered inviting them to my house. It seemed beyond my imagination.

She explained to me the following instructions for the five Archangels to come to your house for five days: First, tidy up your house like you would if you invited friends over. You make a little altar where you place a white candle, a white flower and an apple. Then you write down three wishes—one for yourself, one for your family and friends, and one for the world—and place them in an envelope.

Later in the evening you open your front door and welcome the five Archangels into your home. They stay with you, visiting for five days. At the end of the fifth day, you open the door and thank them as they leave. I thought this was pretty trippy. Previously I had never even considered angels as among my spirit world companions.

Several months later, I invited the five Archangels to come for a visit. I felt blessed by their presence. I invited them to ride with me and come join the art classes that I was teaching. I kept their companionship to myself as I was not quite ready to come out of the closet in regard to my angel buddies.

One of the first things we do in a White Table session is to call in the five Archangels: Michael, Raphael, Gabriel, Uriel, and Metatron, asking their protection. And it seems they respond. Many times during these sessions the mediums have spoken about seeing the Archangels, feeling their wings behind us or being gently lifted up by them.

My artwork is based on my experience with animal spirits, goddess teachers, and my travels in non-ordinary reality. After I had this experience of visiting with the Archangels, I started to look at Renaissance images of Archangel Michael, Archangel Gabriel and Archangel Raphael and learn about their stories. These images of the Archangels influenced my first angel paintings. After I painted several Archangels, I started to paint more personal angels like my dog Izzie, who died several years ago. I painted her as an angel with beautiful wings. Then my spirit dog Cloudy. I included my interest in meditation with my Buddhist spin with the "be here now" angel. Since the Archangels always bring so much love to our White Table ceremonies, love repeatedly appears in my angel paintings like in *angel offering bouquets of love* or *Archangel Gabriel, "all you need is love."*

10 White Table is NOT a *Ouija Board*

Talking to the dead is not a parlor game. Whenever you work with the spirit world, you always need to go with protection and an intention. This is why White Table follows a specific ritual.

Before the mediums arrive, I prepare the room on the day of our monthly White Table. First, I tidy up, getting the room in order. The White Table room is my studio/office when not used for the ceremony. I lay down the white tablecloth, light a candle, and play sacred music softly. The spirits have mentioned that they find the music soothing. The white tablecloth and all the mediums wearing white also have a calming and welcoming effect on the spirits.

Then, when the others arrive, before we even smudge, we write down the names of those who need prayers and love sent—to those who are living and those who are deceased. We have a notebook for these names, which we bring into the ceremony room with us.

Before we enter the room with the white table, we smudge each other with sage smoke to clear any negative energy. Then we do a Brazilian Pass, which is another layer of protection, specifically cleansing the Chakras. Next, we call the spirits of the six directions to create sacred space.

Gathering around the table, we call in the five Archangels: Archangel Michael, Archangel Gabriel, Archangel Raphael, Archangel Uriel, Archangel Metatron. Then each of us silently calls in our power animals and teachers and guides.

We ask the spirits to only bring in those spirits that we can help. This step is vital. You don't want to open the gates of the spirit world and bring anybody who's out there; that's just asking for trouble.

I believe that's what happened when I was in college, doing the Ouija Board with my roommate and a few friends. We were bored and decided to amuse ourselves. Sitting in our dorm room, we started to ask the Ouija Board questions. My roommate and I had our hands resting lightly on the triangular pointer called the planchette.

Suddenly it started spelling out curses and swear words. Another friend freaked out and ran to get the resident house nun. That was it for me and the Ouija Board. I'll stick to playing Monopoly.

Without protection and a specific intention for healing, you may open the gates to all kinds of weird and sometimes scary entities. You want to be cautious and protect yourself and your fellow mediums.

It's essential to have one or more persons at the White Table who are experienced in journeying into the spirit realm. When a spirit does come through, one person asks the questions of the spirit and acts as the primary guide to the Light.

Sometimes what comes up at the table is unpredictable, and not all spirits are easy to work with even when you've asked for only the spirits you can handle. We've discovered that we need to make sure to not only open the circle but at the end to close the circle so that we don't bring spirits home with us.

Another obvious but vital thing is showing up. The spirits know that we've committed to meet with them the first Sunday of every month. It's a commitment, not just to each other but to them. They know and trust us to keep that commitment.

Often at the end of a session we will put on Agua Florida, rose water, or Brigid's holy water for cleansing. Then to ground ourselves afterwards, we have a potluck dinner. It's always a feast—no matter what people bring. The dishes always seem to go together magically—and by the end of the meal people are grounded and ready to return to their homes.

Séances historically have gotten a bad name. In the early 1900s in the United States, there were a lot of con artists who were faking communication with the spirit world to profit from those who were grieving. Knocking sounds, ghostly voices, and levitation of the table were almost always special effects.

White Table has never been part of that sort of con game. There's no knocking or making the table move or staged drama. No one pays to be part of it or to receive messages, and no one makes a profit from these sessions.We're doing it because we feel calledto help the dead cross over and also to receive messages from the spirit world.

11 Talking to the dead, the really dead and the really really dead. What happens in a White Table session?

Each of us took a turn taking notes on the White Table sessions for a while. I include some of the notes from three of these sessions to give the reader an idea of what goes on in White Table.They have been edited for length.

White Table 01.07.2018 Notes taken by Ellen

Opening: Calling in the Archangels and our guides and spirits of the land for protection.

Carol: Thanks to the gathering of grandmothers, goddesses, generations of ancestors, and many animals.We are grateful to them for being here with us.

Erica (groaning and hunched over): I don't feel well.

Pat greets the spirit and asks his name. Answer: Ephra.

Ephra: I don't feel well. It's so cold and I feel like I'm turning to concrete.

(Explains that he's near the subway, and it's bitter cold.) I'm near my maintenance hole, keeping warm there by the subway, but it's painfully cold.

Pat explains that he's died.

Ephra: I feel like I'm still in here.

Pat asks if he can unbend a bit and look up. He does and sees light.Pat asks who might be in the Light who loves him.

Ephra (head bent): Don't know. I left my home and was just living on the streets.

Pat asks if he can bend just a little bit and look up.

Ephra looks. Pat asks who might be in the Light who loves him. No answer. Pat asks how about when he was younger. He says he had brothers and sisters. A special one—Jimmy. Asks if he sees Jimmy. Ephra sees Jimmy's chubby cheeks and freckles.

Ephra asks if Jimmy [and family] will forgive him; he says he took some money.

Pat: We're all about forgiveness here.

She sends him into the Light. *When we ask a soul to meet their loved one in the light, we feel a shift in the room, some of the mediums see a bright light radiating from above, some watch the deceased walk up to their loved ones in the glowing light and disappear.*

Pat: I feel someone pinching my shoulders, especially the right shoulder. (Doesn't know why.)

Erica: Someone is trying to get your attention.Ask who?Man or woman?

[Answer through Pat]: I needed to get your attention and my name is Hal.

Erica: And what's going on with you, Hal?

Hal (confused and indicates that he doesn't trust her): Are you going to give me a lot of jazz?

Erica: If you're here, you're no longer alive and you have a choice to go to the Light, a place of love and healing.

Hal: Don't mind being dead as a doornail, but I don't know about all that light stuff.

Erica: Why don't you try love? There are all these beings around you and they want you to enter the Light with love.

Hal: All these people behind me, pushing me toward light and love?

Erica: Do you see anyone up there (in the Light) who loved you?

Hal: A girl. Sweet. Curls, curly brown hair. Okay, okay. And he goes and disappears into the rays of brilliant light.

Carol: I see a pack of many dogs. A border collie is leading them. They're confused as to where they are. Frozen to death in storms and don't know where to go. When I talk to the border collie, she's not saying anything; she just wants to know where to go.

Pat: I wonder if we can call on some of our beloved dogs who have died to come down and lead the way to the Light.

Carol explains to border collie/dogs that we are bringing friends from the Light, who will show them the way home and lead the way across the Rainbow Bridge.

Erica: There's someone there handing out milk bones, getting them going, leaping, and prancing. Other dogs are coming, more and more.

Erica: I'm seeing one dog, an Airedale.

Airedale: You think cold is terrible? I was left in a car.

Erica: He wants some loving too. His name is Arthur. Go follow the other ones, Arthur.

Pat: I see a group of angels who are flying around us. They have balls of light. They are flying around the table, going, "Duck, duck, goose" with balls of light. [They are putting those balls of light] in our heads through our crown chakra. The light stays there and gets to emanate out, because we are light bearers and it [the light] is there for us. Call on these angels and ask them to charge our crown chakras with the light if there are any dark nights of the soul. They're saying they like how the Renaissance artists depicted them, especially the northern European Renaissance artists.

Erica: People whose names we wrote down for prayers, the angels are infusing them with healing light.

Sophia: Jimmy is here. In the woods.

Lucinda: What is he doing in the woods?

Sophia: It's hard for him to breathe.

Lucinda: Why is it hard to breathe?

Sophia: He's hurt. It's hard for him to walk, and he's dragging himself through woods.

Lucinda: What happened to him?

Sophia: I think a war. Uniform, leather belt. But no one is with him.

Lucinda: Well, the angels are with him, and we're here to support him as well. You can ask him if he would like to go to the Light and join the loved ones waiting for him there.

Sophia asks and says that he's shaking his head, yes.

Lucinda: Jimmy, look up and see someone you loved in your life. There's someone there with a hand outstretched for you.

Sophia: Yes, he's anxious to go.

Lucinda: All he has to do is reach out and fly free.

Sophia: He's reaching out. And he's gone.

Dawn: I've been seeing a man wandering through a graveyard. He said his name is Harold, and he's really sick and has never believed in anything after death. Now he's suffering, dead, wandering around in a graveyard, and doesn't know what to do.

Pat: Can you tell him to look up for the Light?

Dawn: I've been telling him but he's so strong in believing that nothing's there that he can't see it.

Pat: Well, why don't we just send him love and maybe that will shift.

Dawn: He says he feels warmer.

Pat: We're just going to send him love and it's going to lift him up.Can he see anyone now?

Dawn: Yes, he sees his parents, and it looks like he's headed in that direction.

Pat: That's right, Harold, go to them now.

Pat: I have a sense that Don Pedro is sitting next to me with his hands on table. He was a friend and a medicine man I worked with who died of a heart attack several years ago. But I need help chatting him up because I don't know if it's time for him to go to the Light. But he likes the energy of this room and appreciates the work that we are all doing at the White Table.

Erica: How are you?

Don Pedro [through Pat]: I like it here. I wasn't ready to die.So I've been drifting around in the sacred spaces that my friends create.

Erica: Do you feel you don't want to leave [because of the people here]?

Don Pedro: No. I just like drifting around these liminal spaces.

Erica: Well, you know there are many kinds of liminal spaces. Have you been to other types of sacred spaces—others forms, more ethereal and spiritual? [He was a Sun dancer many times and had led many sweat lodges.]

Don Pedro: When you go to the Light, you lose your personality.

Erica: Well, there might be other personalities, though your essence goes on. Is there anything you want to say to Pat?

Don Pedro: I love her dearly, but she doesn't need me. Other helping spirits and ancestors surround her. Archangels Michael and Gabriel, it's a good crowd.I like hanging out here.

Erica: After you do the work you need to do, you can come back here and hang out with these spirits. Are you willing [to go to the Light]?

Don Pedro: Let's do it.

Erica: On you go.

Erica: I'm just seeing so many people with great sadness. They lost their will to live because times have been so challenging for them this year.Things they loved are changing; feel like the ground is being yanked out from under them. They are choosing to leave by dying.

Pat: Do they need help?

Erica: I'm seeing a band of foggy greyness.Many chose to leave through sickness, flu. It's a like a radio band that they are stuck in. It's hurting our atmosphere on earth. So if we can ask the angels . . .

Pat: If we connect with the web of light, it can lift them up.And if we can sense the balls of light that came inside us, we can send it [the light] out to lift them up.

Annemarie: Lots of rainbow light.

Annemarie [Don Pedro is speaking through her, in Spanish, and she is translating]: For those that don't believe in climate change.There's a problem, many people unconscious still.

Erica [amused]: Would you like to stay for the rest of the evening and then leave?

Annemarie: He says he's not the only male. [Annemarie asks, Who else is here?]

Don Pedro: The father of Susan is here and wants to beg for forgiveness.

Susan: He has it.

Annemarie: We have to help [him] back to Light, but he wants to tell Susan he's really sorry if he hurt her, but it wasn't on purpose.

Susan: I forgive him.

Annemarie: Who else is here, Don Pedro?

Don Pedro: The blond brother. He's still here, and he's not ready. Be strong and forgive him, Lucinda.

Lucinda: I do. I love you, Dave.

Don Pedro: He loves you so much, and he's just not ready to let go. Don Pedro is with him. Don't fear for him; be happy for him; that's what will make it easy. He's going to go. He's going.

Carol: One man who is here is Charles (Pat's deceased husband and art partner). He's just stopping to say, "Hi, Pat."

Pat: Good to see you, Charles.

Charles (through Carol): Bye, Pat.

Pat: Maybe there's an online dating site for people who only have relationships with spirits.

Pat: I see Erica's father, and I see his hands.He so loves you.

Erica: There was never a time I didn't love him.

Pat: He's sorry about things that happened with the community. He didn't know what to do but thought she handled herself with so much wisdom and grace.

Erica: Thank you, Dad.

Pat: He loves you and is there for you now, the way he was there for you when you were a little girl. He admires the way you are as a mother and will be there with you for whatever comes now.

Erica: Do you see my brother Bertil?

Pat: I see a tiny cherub, a relative of the whistling angel. A tiny mite.

Erica's father (through Pat): That was an unfortunate thing that happened to Mother. But you do not have to feel guilty about any of that. It was not your doing at all. You were such a shining light, a baby who exuded light.

Pat: And he felt powerless when he saw people trying to tamp that light down, but that's not the case now.

Erica: You were a remarkable father.

Erica: Does he see my mother, Marianne?

Pat: No, he doesn't see her. It's a different ball game over there. Just because you're connected in this life, not necessarily connected there. He's reaching out his hands to you, and anytime you're frightened, just reach out your hands and he is there to hold yours.

Annemarie: The table suddenly got warm.

Pat: The spirit guides here are grateful for the notes. People must have this information. Not New Age, more profound than that, and not letting it slip away.

Carol: Do they have suggestions on how we're to share it?

Erica: I'm getting "a blog."

Pat: I'm getting, "Speak it." What do we name it? Cross with me? Come on Over? White Table Blog?

Ellen: I have a question for the spirits. Can we be open about all of this without being attacked for it?

Annemarie: No.

Pat: But we're strong enough to handle it, not as individuals but as a collective. Now more than ever, this needs to be spoken around with intensity of Me Too. A spiritual Me Too, and all ancestors burned at stake or punished are here supporting us. They have our backs, and they're here for us.

Erica: It's about giving this away like precious pearls. Not being sensational. When someone needs a precious pearl, you give it to them and they receive it.

Carol: If care is taken, resistance will be less. Discreet.

Annemarie: Lots of blessings from many, many souls.

Erica: We're each supposed to gather blessings around us like a cloak or shawl and when we leave here, we will still be wrapped in blessings.

Pat: I keep seeing Abraham Lincoln. He had to speak his truth but he wasn't protected.And we are. And he's very proud that we're willing to speak our truth at this time in history.From a place of compassion, love.

Susan: I'm getting all the spirits of all the women who have gone before us. A phalanx of people, crowds and crowds, layers. They have our backs. And everything that's happening is all right. It's when we're called upon for our ethics to be sharp and to be blessed with all the energy coming in from our ancestors and the past. We're lucky. To be living in this time. I don't know if they need to go to Light or are angels.

Erica: Ask.

[Answer through Susan]: No, we're from the Light. [Annemarie got the same answer.]

Annemarie: Getting a real loud message—The only thing we have to fear is fear itself. [Minor debate over whether that was Churchill or FDR.]

Erica: We want to thank all these men for coming through. It takes a lot of chutzpah with all these women.

Susan: Do you think he'll [Don Pedro] come back?

Erica: Oh yeah.

Annemarie: He says he never left.

Dawn: Feels to me like he comes back from the Light a lot.

Annemarie: There really is no division. Just a crossing.

Pat: So is it necessary to go to the Light?

Susan: The Light is in us.

Erica: That expression . . . we're not bodies with souls inside, but we're souls with bodies.

Pat: Maybe if we had more of a sense of that, death wouldn't be so scary, because the soul is constantly moving back and forth, like an infinity symphony.

Pat: Dancing and moving in the body is also connecting to spirit. Dancing is a way that you can be in your body and in the spirit world at the same time.

Carol: It's getting quiet for everyone.

Erica: Yes, the veil between the worlds just closed.

Annemarie: Thanks to all the spirits, Archangels, ancestors, wisdom teachers, animals, and nature for being with us and guiding us.Anything we need to close the sacred circle? All of us holding hands and feeling the light stream through us.

Ellen: I just got that in Renaissance paintings of Jesus where he's holding a crystal ball, the sphere is supposed to symbolize the world, but what he was actually carrying was one of those balls of light that the angels sent into us.

Aren't we the lucky ones.

I Believe in Miracles

White Table 12.2.201 Notes by Pat

Erica: Archangels, please place a pyramid of light around us and make our hearts open.

Ellen: Guardian angels and animal spirits, please help those on the border.

Erica: Compassionate spirits of place.

Pat: I call upon the spirits of our ancestors.

Dawn: Open our hearts and fill them with love.

Ellen: Sending blessings for people who are helping on the border

Erica: Allow us to be above the level of differences and work in non-bias.

Pat: My grandma, Velma is here, sporting wings. She says to step up, that we are recalibrating, and getting younger. Pat, draw angels.

Annemarie: My mom is here. Pat, you could be very famous and have a huge market for drawing angels. There is a vast market.

Annemarie needs to start writing. Don't worry about money.

Annemarie is lucky to have Pat and Susan and all the women.

Thank you. Be grateful. Enjoy.

Erica: When we eat or experience comfort, we are doing it for people who don't have that. Appreciate for them what they don't have.

Erica: The conductors—I see conductor spirits—they come in and out, experiencing the music, and it brings them joy.

Pat: The images we put in our brains are significant. Also we need to step up and say we are doing it.

Erica: I am hearing, "Open your crown chakra for healing." It's an exquisite color of gold. The mycelium that connects the trees—we can use that net to send light. That's why we feel at home.

We are connected by mycelium. Places love us.

Dawn: I am reminded that as we age we have more people on the other side, and it makes it easier to tune in.

Pat: If we make it an intention, we can have loved ones come in dreams.

Pat: It keeps being vital that we talk about the work that we do.

Annemarie: I fear being called witches

Erica: I hear that we are being filled up.

Annemarie: There's an old woman in a rocking chair related to one of us. She is confused. Help her. She needs love.

Pat: Does she know she's dead? Look up at the radiant light. There's no hell, no burning, just love, beautiful light.

Annemarie: [in the voice of the woman] I'm leaving.

Dawn: I have to take a break from news. It's easier to send love.

Pat: Doing Metta while swimming helps. Each time is like a drop that makes a difference.

Pat's Metta:

> May all beings be safe
> May all beings be happy
> May all beings be healthy
> May all beings live in peace

Annemarie: I see angels dancing. Of course there is hope. Paint them, Pat.

Annemarie: The church of love. The key, like St. Peter's. Boy, these angels are good looking. There is a multitude of angels.

Pat: Patrick drew a picture of us when Charles died. He was six and put angel wings on all of us.

Annemarie: Susan, your grandmother is here. She wants you to know she is so proud of you. You have turned out beyond her wildest dreams, and she is always with you.

There's a man with a feather in his head. He hears our prayers for rain. Strong water is coming. Collect it if you can. Rivers will flow. Let Izzie in. She is a spirit dog now.

(Izzie was my hound dog, who died a year before this White Table session.)

Annemarie: The answer to everything is love.

White Table Notes 8.12.18 Witnessed by Sophia

We are naming those in our thoughts and prayers.

Blessing, opening, an invitation to helpers and guides, and calling in protection.

Erica: Izzie's here, sniffing and licking, nose in lap. Tail is going wop, wop, wop.

(Izzie is Pat's coon hound, who died recently.)

Pat: Miss you, Izzie Lou, sweet, sweet Izzie.

Erica: She's thankful to you for the measures you took for her. She's so devoted to you and grateful for all you gave to her.

Pat: She's my guardian hound dog now.

Erica: She wants you to go out and bay when you need to. She says we all have that much love in our eyes, just let the love come out of your eyes if you're feeling shy or see someone who is down and out.

Annemarie: She's with a bunch of puppies. She would have stayed longer if she could have.

Erica: [Izzie says that] Feliz (Pat's tuxedo cat) wasn't bad as cats go. She's glad that you have Feliz.

Pat: There's still a big part in my heart for Izzie.

Dawn: I loved that she'd greet each of us when we came in.

Pat: I have a sense that the psilocybin mushrooms are here. I ingested them the night before Izzie died and they're saying I should try to draw the images they gave me and not to be freaked out by the intensity of the experience.

Erica: I keep being shown that we each have etheric crowns with lights around them held together with etheric filaments. They're meant to help us receive and transmit to the other dimensions. Tonight is the Perseid meteor showers -- a significant time to cosmic download. The Perseids are necessary for what they're dispensing through the atmosphere.Connect with them before you go to bed, but they will still affect you.

Annemarie asks for healing energy for herself and for all of us, the planet, and those suffering.

Bless our children and grandchildren and all the generations.

Annemarie feels lots of tingling in her hands.All agree they feel tingling too.

Annemarie: Two little blond kids fighting over a book.It's hot, and they're moving and screaming and crying, and the house is on fire, and they're going to be dead very soon. They're tiny, crawling under the bed.

Erica: Where are their parents?

Annemarie: Don't know, two doves are now flying. They're gone, their souls are going to the Light. Their parents are watching, and they're all together now. They're watching us too.

Erica: Is that happening now? Yes, from [the wildfires in] CA maybe.

Annemarie: They're joining a lot of people. All the little bodies are red.

Erica asks if Annemarie wants to breathe it out and let it go, as it's hard to see that.

Annemarie: I just saw these forest spirits--cedar and oak. They did a smudging on my family—a whirlwind of energy going up, and it took away a lot of bad stuff.They're the spirits of the trees but they feel angelic.

Lucinda: They enjoyed your family and want the best for them.What a gift.

Dawn: I've been having images of animals fleeing from the fires.They run and it catches up to them, and they run more and get stuck by fences by the freeways.

Annemarie: Someone's on my right shoulder, a woman.Mary Anne. I think someone hit me, [Mary Anne says].It hurts a lot. He hit me with a big stick.

Pat asks her to go to the Light.

Annemarie: [speaking for Mary Anne] I see a sparkly sun. My kids, my mom is there, and my papa. Let's go and go into the Light.

Pat: Spirits are reminding that this circle of love and light is always available to us. We just have to remember.It can envelop us, and we can wrap ourselves in this energy to remind us that we are loved and loving.

Dawn: Feels like it grows as we pull it into ourselves and send it back out to everyone.

Erica: I keep being reminded that those in our lives who are our greatest challenge are also our greatest gift—to teach us how to love and grow.

Annemarie: Someone is here for Susan. He's walking and jumping. And there's a horse. Carol's horse, Ben

Pat: Barney [Carol's dog] is with Ben and watching out for him. Let Carol know that Barney and Ben are playing. And they both really appreciate her love and dedication to both of them. And they both think it's great that she's retired now and not to worry.

Annemarie: I think there's someone on the ground.A man is crying by a plane. The plane crashed and he's feeling bad. I think his name is Peter.

Ellen: He stole the plane and crashed it.

Annemarie: [speaking for Peter] Did I die?

Pat: It's okay, there is no judgment.You're in a place of love.We help people cross over to the Light. Look up and you can go there. In that light is someone who loved you.

Annemarie [speaking for Peter]: My mother is there. Thank you.

Pat: The whistling cherub is back to bring some cheer! Whistling, singing and hand dancing occurs.

Dawn: I've been feeling my brother [Danny] next to me the whole time. He says we all have too much fun doing this. He had a good sense of humor. He's nudging me to share that I felt him next to me in my recliner this week. He drags as many family members along to visit as he can. He's interested in life after death, mediums, ghosts.

Erica: I want to ask Danny if he thinks there's a difference between ghosts and spirits.

Dawn: Ghosts are those who haven't been able to go into the Light and spirits are the ones who have.

Erica: Question for Danny—Do ghosts' energy diminish over time?

Dawn: He's not too sure but he'll ponder it.They exist not in time.

Erica: But they're attached to houses or people.

Dawn: He says nothing is permanent so that attachment will fade

Susan: Annemarie, your mom wants me to watch over you.

Annemarie: She says your dad is having a great time. And so is your mom. Your mom dances all the time, and she knows we all dance and move.

Erica: Because we were in our mother's womb and mother was in grandmother's, that's why our mothers and grandmothers stay with us in the spirit world because our mother/grandmother was carrying our soul.Like Russian dolls within each other, and they embrace us.It upsets the balance if a daughter goes before the mother or grandmother.

Erica: I'm having a strange feeling—there is something on my back—monkey on my back . Any addiction is called a monkey on my back.These are spirits too. This person is wrestling with this spirit. Like tentacles. It's getting dark. It's a vision of how addiction works, with little tentacles that go into body and they're in an awful, wrestling match all the time. Love needs to be sent to these people who are suffering from addiction. "It's so hard to win."We can help Tomas by sending him, love. He has swarthy skin and black hair.

Ellen: Maybe if we visualize the tentacles dissolving.

Erica: This was showing us what addiction is like. Tomas feels sticky. Tomas, what do you need?

Luce: How about an Archangel? St. Michael—can you cut this man free?

Erica says she needs to have her back cleansed; it feels like a ladder is on her back.

We all put some light on Erica.

Luce saw Erica carrying a lot of energy and debris from a family gathering, which allowed these spirits to attach to her

Erica: Also going to Airbnb's and hotels, we have to ask for protection. Spirits are everywhere.

The session ends with the sounds of a cleansing rain on the roof. Thank you.

Be Here Now Angel

12 Getting to know you ... Meet the White Table Mediums

When I began writing this book, I thought it would be essential to hear from the other eight mediums. I enjoy interviewing my friends, so this was easy and fun. I asked them the following four questions: What drew you to the White Table work? What have you learned doing White Table? What gifts have you received from our White Table community? How do you receive the spirits—hearing, seeing, physical presence in your body, other? Not everyone answered the questions exactly as I asked them, but everyone gave me a sense of their White Table experience. Here's what they said:

Sophia

What have you learned doing White Table?

We are all learning about what is really important. How much of ourselves and what we believe is an illusion. After my mother died, she told me the conflicts were an illusion. It was our resistance that kept the conflict [between us] alive. Had we been able to get through the resistance, we could have changed things between us earlier.

Through the communications with my grandmother in White Table, I have been realizing how much support I have from my grandmother and great-grandmother. Now with my mother who now is in the spirit world, I can feel more support from her than I did when she was alive. I feel the support from the three of them, and then the maternal lineage that goes back even further. I really had not felt that before doing the White Table work. It's super profound as if it has altered the way I can be in the world, really feeling into the support. I went through a lot of my life thinking that I don't have a lot of support.

After these experiences of support from my mother, grandmother, and great grandmother, they showed up on the dance floor. We were arm in arm, the four of us in a circle. We were just dancing to this one song. I, of course, was sobbing. It was one of the most beautiful experiences I've ever had.

Sophia's Story

My Grandmother Mildred, my mother's mother, helped me with the transition of my mother's death through White Table.Without this communication and support from the other side, my experience of my mother's death would have been very different, and I may have felt somewhat alone in it. Instead, my grandmother and I were in this together -- with me taking care of my mother here on earth and my grandmother ready to receive my mother in the spirit world. My grandmother and I supported each other, and this experience allowed me to be more present and compassionate with my mother in her final months. I am so grateful for this guidance, love and support from the other side by my grandmother. This experience changed my life.

During a White Table session in April 2019, my Grandmother Mildred visits and tells me, "It's okay, it's all going to be okay." I wonder, is my mother dying?

Later in May 2019, again during a White Table session, my Grandmom Mildred is present and wants me to let my mother know that it's okay, she will be waiting for her when she is ready. When she's too tired, it's okay to let go. Grandmom isn't sure she can access Mom. But I can let Mom know that I had a dream and Grandmom let me know that she is waiting for her when she is ready and that all is going to be okay.

My grandmother relates that she would have liked to do this work but didn't have access to it or it wouldn't have been understood by others in her life.Erica says that Mildred is welcome here and everyone agrees--she can be with us anytime. Mildred loves this.She is thrilled and grateful to be here and to be included in this work. Mildred relays that she is thrilled to have access to me in this way. I am so grateful for this way to communicate with her and for us to be there for one another.

Five days later my mother is ill and I will be taking her to the hospital.Before we go, we sit and talk and hold hands. I let her know that Grandmother/her mother, has visited me in a dream and wants her to know that it's okay, she will be waiting for her when she's ready to leave this world as she knows it. Mildred will be there waiting for her.We cry together.I ask if she is ready to die and she says no.

My mother died on June 30, 2019.It was her decision to leave and not continue to live in a body that did not allow her to live her life fully and freely. Her heart was tired and her heart was sad.

A month later, I had an image come through during our White Table session, in the silence and the rain, of my grandmother, Mildred. I've been processing the image as it was profound and she didn't speak to me, but I knew there was so much in this image to explore.

She was asleep and she was floating in the ocean. The image was cropped close to her head and she appeared younger than when she died. The lighting was a beautiful, sweet light, warm and flat, at the end of the day that is so beautiful on the skin. The feeling was one of peace and rest as she was floating in the calm and slowly undulating water. The water felt like the water of life and the message that comes to me is, "The work is done, you can rest."

I have the sense that my grandmother can be here for me now, in a more full way than when my mother was alive. My grandmother and I took care of my mom and it felt like we were both helping her to transition — with me on this side being with my mom at the end of life and my grandmother on that side. Even coming through me to let my mom know she was there for her, waiting, and all would be okay. It was such a gift for me to be able to share that with my mother after receiving that at White Table months ago. So now, with this image from Sunday, I have the sense that I can rest now and my grandmother is with me and I have the resource of this feeling of deep peace and restfulness that I can use as a resource whenever I need it.

The other feeling/message I have from this image is the feeling of "in between" and the sense that transitioning from this realm to the next can be like floating in the Water of Life. Peacefully floating between both worlds and then floating to the next calmly and unhurriedly—peacefully. My grandmother was in a medically induced coma at the end of her life and I have the sense that this is how she did that transition, floating in and out until she was ready to fully move on from this realm. In being with my Mother during that last month and at the time of her passing, it felt the same way, so floaty, restful and peaceful. I now have the sense that this was the message my grandmother wanted to relay to and through me to share with my mother, that "it will all be okay, don't worry, I'm here - and Sophia is there on that side." In this way, my grandmother and I were both crossing guards, with me releasing my mother's hand into my grandmother's hand.

I want to add at the end of my story that about an hour before my mother stopped breathing, she called out "Mama." I knew then that my grandmother was here to help her go to the other side. I breathed a sigh and welcomed her and cried. I knew my mother was safe and taken care of.

Lucinda

What drew you to the White Table work?

You, Erica, and I were journeying weekly to the spirits. I found these experiences very profound. Then you told us about the mediums from Brazil coming again to California to teach a workshop on White Table, learning how to be a medium and healing deceased souls. This was the workshop that you had attended four years earlier. I was attracted to attending the workshop; it sounded like another aspect of what we had been doing with journeys. I wanted to learn more and deepen my knowledge and practice. After the workshop, I was opened to working more with the spirits, and I felt more sensitive. I felt it was like an initiation.

What have you learned doing White Table?

Reality isn't what I thought it was. There is the seen and the unseen. That there is the unseen life, which is as powerful and real as what we see and touch. That was a big learning. I kind of knew that intellectually, but this way I experienced it viscerally. It changed my perspective of my day-to-day life. I am with spirits all the time. I walk into my house and say "Hi, everybody! I'm home!" I feel blessed. Before the White Table work, I would have never done that.

What gifts have you received from our White Table community?

Beautiful friendship. I never would have met some of these women. I have tremendous respect for the women we work with. They augment my life. Many humans living in this technical life that we live in, have lost that sensitivity to what is around them.

How do you receive the spirits? Hearing, seeing, physical presence in your body, other?

I hear them and, in my mind, I see them. The first time we did White Table with Zoom, a guy showed up shouting "Help me! I've been waiting for you! I was told you'd be here at this time every month!" I told him I was sorry—we had not been meeting because of Covid—but we are here now. He was frantic. He knew he was stuck but he didn't know how to undo that. I see people in my mind and see what they are wearing, to get us to see when and where they are from.

I feel that each of us have our own personality and vessel. We are going to perceive the world and those in it in our own way. My connection to the spirit world is not limited to one Sunday afternoon at White Table. As a practicing Herbalist, when I go out to look for particular plants to make medicine, I call in the spirit of that particular plant.

Carol

What have you learned doing White Table?

My experience with White Table affirmed an alternate reality and the plausibility of communicating in that dimension. I have also learned the power of doing it together.

In White Table it is almost visual how we create the circuit connecting the nine of us, our hands are on the table, our feet are on the ground. We are in a circle and you can viscerally feel it flowing through us.

Since Covid, we are doing White Table virtually via Zoom. We are getting information on how to navigate now in the world.

How do you receive the spirits? Hearing, seeing, physical presence in your body, other?

Occasionally I feel the spirits, then physically, often in the beginning of a White Table session, I will feel Ben behind me, playing with my hair. Ben is a horse of mine who has passed away. Mostly I see and sense. He's kind of my spirit horse, who also shows up in my shamanic journeys. He has primarily been my grieving horse. He takes me through grief. Also, other animals who have passed come through me, for example, Pat's coon hound Izzie. A couple of my dogs have come as well. A couple of years ago, Molly, my black dachshund, came to White Table, confused, and lost. She didn't know where she was. We called upon some of her animal friends who were on the other side to come and get her. Ben came to get her. When Ben was alive, Molly would come with me to visit Ben, so they knew each other. She followed Ben up to the Light.

Annemarie

What have you learned doing White Table?

What drew me to the White Table was the women who were participating. I always had these philosophical questions: "Where did we come from? Where are we going? Why are we here?" My mother practiced Spiritism even though she was a devout Catholic. Maybe I was drawn to White Table to answer the almost unanswerable question, "What happens when we die?"

Have some of these questions been answered doing the White Table?

I've learned that it is a good thing to assist spirits. I believe the only reality is love. Although I had to practice my conservative Catholicism, I was always looking to manifest goodness and love in the world. The White Table is a very selfless way to do that. My first answers to these philosophical questions was existentialism. The general thinking in the world is once you die, that's it. The older I get the less afraid I get. Consorting with the spirits gives you a lot of freedom.

How do you receive the spirits? Hearing, seeing, physical presence in your body, other?

In White Table the way I experience the spirits is first physically in my skin or I feel someone tap my shoulder then I start seeing things like a movie. Often the spirits will say to me, "Tell them what I am saying to you." I don't know how I know; I just know. One time Spinoza came through and told me to read his writings. He also told us to whistle while we pray and to merge with the goddesses. I used to be afraid of my mother but now she is in the spirit world, I call on her all the time. She is very supportive of me doing this work. Sometimes when I hear a song and listen, I go into a trance and then something will be revealed to me. One time, it was Mom, and she had a message for my daughter Natalia. It is a such a blessing to be of service. It is so peaceful when I am doing it.

Susan

What have you learned doing White Table?

I think the main thing I learned was to trust my intuition because we live in a culture that puts down things that we cannot see. Our culture believes that this reality, its physicality, is real. I felt when I first came to White Table that I was not very good at this compared to some of the other women. But I always have been very psychic. Some of us have had more practice. A big piece for me was to say to myself, *if you don't get much that's okay. Just go with it and trust your intuition.* Being together creates the circle of energy that makes it all happen. I think everybody is connected to the spirit world in their own souls.

Another gift is just being with the spirits. I also never thought that much about the Archangels. Now I really feel their presence more. I also did the thing where you invite the Archangels to come to your house for five days to visit and bless you and your home. So being more tuned into the Archangel realm is a gift as well.

Another important aspect of White Table is the synchronicity that we all will experience even the same words, and the same visions. For me that is very validating for the whole experience.

How do you receive the spirits?

I would hear something, but it wasn't exterior, more an interior voice. It's sort of a feeling and a hearing. I couldn't think that I was manufacturing it but even so, it is a part of the gestalt of reality. We are cocreating with not just God but with all of each other. To believe you're making it up is going into your head and blocking off your intuition. I thought the time Annemarie talked to Spinoza was really interesting. Lately I have had reoccurring dreams about friends who are dead, and I think those people are trying to communicate with me.

What has stood out to me is the Zoom calls since Covid and not being physically together is just as powerful, if not more powerful, than being there in person. Again, it validates the whole thing that there is no space or time. You don't have to be in a room with someone to be connected with them. No space. No time. Between your world and the spirit world, is like a very thin veil.

Ellen

What drew you to the White Table work?

I was invited by Lucinda and Erica. It was just after my mom died, and I was having a hard time with it. I think they invited me as a way to help me with my grief. It helped me but not directly as I haven't had that many direct messages from my mother.

What have you learned doing White Table?

Indirectly, through White Table, I have begun to feel better about death and life, and the spirit world. I feel like I am the least psychic person in the group, as I don't get a whole lot of spirits speaking to me. But I have had a few who have died come to me and it's always surprised me. And I've seen proof of other people offered specific messages that turned out to be very valuable and true. It has made me believe that yes, there is something beyond this life as we know it. One of the pieces I got is that when you die, some part of you goes on. It's not necessarily a reflection of your physical being here. It might be much more abstract than that. I also found that because it's bound by love, the spirit can take on a form that can give information to you. In other words, it could take another form. It can appear in ways to help us. It can go back and forth from an abstract energy form to someone you recognize.

What gifts have you received from our White Table community?

There is a certain intensity when we are all around the table and the physical vibration of the people in the room. When we do it in our own homes and then gather on Zoom, it keeps our connection going which I think is very important. I love the feasts of amazing food that we share and the friendship of these women, who are all extraordinary in their own right. I have really enjoyed getting to know them. It's a very unique community. We didn't know each other before and nowI feel like we are a group with strong ties. It is a special part of my life.

I grew up in a Jewish family and went through twelve years of Hebrew School. I decided I didn't want to practice Judaism because I had trouble with the jealous, vengeful God of the Old Testament. And yet I love the angels. This is a spirituality that is embracing of other traditions and is so open that it works for me. I also see it as a spiritual practice. Traditional Judaism is pretty existential. You live and you die.

Erica

What drew you to the White Table work?

I have always been interested in communication with spirits and the fact that the spirits are with us all the time. They are in another dimension interacting with us and watching over us. I have learned more by listening to other people channel souls than myself. I have been so astonished by what comes through. This is when we are sitting at White Table and being mediums for different spirits who come through individual mediums. If ever there was a little bit of doubt that this was real, it vanishes when someone brings through things that they couldn't possibly have known. Like when Spinoza came through Annmarie, when she only knew his name. She brought through all this information that when we checked it out was spot on.

When we first started doing White Table, I absolutely thought I was making it up. I wouldn't call it stage fright, but a feeling that I wouldn't be able to do it. That doesn't happen anymore.

In my art and poetry, the spirits come through. I think this work of White Table and the spirits is particularly important at this time of the pandemic. There is the possibility of bringing so much peace, solace, and answers for people, all over, who are in fear, terror, pain, distress, and grief. We are being given an opportunity to sit and bring through this information. And you, Pat, are being tapped to record it all.

It is important that someone is doing this work somewhere. This information needs to be shared. All of us are out in the world in different ways. We are not crazy, we are grounded. The more we can share it with people like, "Oh yeah! This happened. Today we talked to the spirits." It normalizes it for people. The more you talk to people, the more you realize that they are absolutely open and accepting. I think everybody has had experiences like this that they keep closeted away. I think everybody who has had someone they loved die, hopes they'll get some kind of a sign. They mostly don't tell people that it was a butterfly.

Remote WhiteTable June 5, 2022 Erica's notes, while holding a "channeling crystal"

People who died were taken by guides in a golden boat with wings. It floated on a river of tears from those who mourned the passengers. The boat passed through an archway of crystalline matter made from the tears of the mourners. It had solid substance but was not a permanent structure.

The boat lifted up and rose to a gathering space. People were sent in groups of 10 to 20 to be with guides or angelic beings who spoke to them about where they were. The newly arrived were purified by hand motions similar to the Brazilian Pass. Each spirit was given a memory box and sent to a serene spot to open it. They were encouraged to sift through their memories and create something from them to transform the memories. Some beings planted gardens, some wrote poems ornpainted or made songs or danced. Some knitted shawls and placed them on the shoulders of the grieving (etherically). People had access to scales and could see that all memories had equal weight and value.

The arrivals could sit with a holy person or guide if they desired and be scanned. Ranks and hierarchies and egos were stripped away. There was a laughter room to release the seriousness of the life lived. One could request a viewing in the consequence room to see what effects their actions had on others. It felt similar to the review Scrooge endures in A Christmas Carol.

There was a communication room. One purpose of the room was to be able to communicate intuitively with pets.

Later: People need to learn about radiance and life force. As elements like water and clean air and food become scarcer, we need to learn to appreciate and discern the life force that we ingest and that sustains us. Gratitude is the key. Less food or fuel is necessary if we pay attention to the essence of what we use.

Dawn

What drew you to the White Table work?

From early childhood I had many dreams and intuitive experiences that others around me didn't seem to understand or give importance to as I did. My mother even used to tell me not to talk about that stuff as it might make people think I was a crazy.That taught me to be quiet and question my feelings as a kid.

The first memory I have of seeing a dead person in this lifetime was when I was about six years old. Our neighbor had died by suicide. Before we heard about it, I was out in the backyard with my mother and saw a translucent figure wearing a white suit and a top hat.As I recall, I asked my mother if she saw what I saw. She had not.

My paternal grandmother (Lilly) attended seances in the 1950s. Most of the family thought she was a little strange. That also signaled me that seeing or hearing the dead was weird.

For as long as I can remember, I've been able to feel the presence of deceased loved ones. When my mother died, she came to me and told me not to be sad, that she was fine and never far from me. Although I grieved, seeing my mother helped me get through the loss. After my dad died, he came to me in a dream, wearing a black suit and top hat. (He never dressed like that during his life.)

He told me that he was very happy in the Spirit world and that he could have one beer a day, which was all he needed. I shared these experiences with my family including my brother Danny. He was always interested in contacting people after their death. A few days before Danny's death he told me that he envied me, that I had this sense of our parents, as he had never been able to feel their presence.

What gifts have you received from our White Table community?

The greatest gift is the degree to which I've learned to trust and use my intuition, which in turn has enabled it to become stronger. The intimacy and friendships with the White Table group are truly blessings to me as well. There is such a powerful feeling of being there for each other. We nourish each other's spirits. Sometimes more than one of us will experience the same things. It never ceases to amaze me. For example, once we were doing White Table outside by Pat's fishpond. I felt a cat rubbing on my leg. I did not mention it, but finally opened my eyes and looked. There was no physical cat in sight. A minute later Ellen, who was sitting to my left said, "I'm feeling a cat rubbing on my leg."

Is there an experience at White Table that impacted your life?

White Table has confirmed that my experiences with those who had crossed over are real and need never to be questioned.I now recognize the reality of my experiences with the spirit world and am comfortable enough to talk about them with those who are sincerely interested.

As a Reiki practitioner I send Reiki to those who have crossed over and send healing to my ancestors.

Dawn's Story

On August 8, 2017 in the early afternoon, my phone rang. The news came, my brother Danny was dead. My life would be forever changed.

After the call, I sat down to meditate with the hope of connecting to my brother. I began talking with Danny, who had left his body behind only a few hours earlier. He was now in the Spirit realm. "You could not bear the pain anymore. Maybe if the pain were only physical . . . or only emotional. . . Or if you had felt supported in the way you needed to be. I will not get caught in 'should haves' or 'what ifs.' The choice was yours. It took courage. A new chapter begins for us both. I celebrate your freedom yet grieve that I will never see you again in the body, as the brother that I have so dearly loved. Emotions run deep. Time will make the wound less painful, and I know we will have many encounters, you as Spirit, me as aging sister incarnate. Most of all, I do not want my sadness to dampen your joy of being where you have long desired to be. So talk to me when it feels right ... and again, please don't let my grief limit your happiness ..."

I felt his presence immediately. He didn't want me to be sad. A few hours later, I noticed that he had sent me a private message on Facebook, shortly before his death saying, "I love you."

That first night after his death, Danny came to visit me in an incredibly vivid dream. He wanted me to know that he was so glad to be free of all that troubled him. He felt blessed to be back with those he held so dear, who crossed over before him, our parents, grandparents, some friends, and his cat Gracie. He told me he could be anywhere he wanted to be, and all he had to do was think of a place. He showed me that he was in downtown Tucson joyfully roaming the streets. We both know that dying by suicide does not bring about eternal damnation, as some believe. Sometimes lessons get to be too much for one life. When the spirit is ready to reincarnate, there will be opportunities to work through them later.

That visit gives me solace to this day. I am so grateful that I can communicate with the Spirit world. White Table has both validated and strengthened my ability. Frequently, I feel my brother near me. He always joins me at White Table and sits at my right. Many of my family, friends, and animal companions also join me during White Table. I have a host of ancestors, who sit with me like a field of Buddhas stretching out beside and behind me.

Angel Resists Being Hoodwinked

13 The spirits enroll me to be their scribe? Really?

I was informed that I was to be their scribe in a visit with my spirit teachers—a council of six kickass goddesses. They include Brigid, a goddess from ancient Ireland. She is associated with wisdom, poetry, healing and protection and was my first teacher. Then Danu, the mother goddess of the ancient tribe of the Tuatha De Danann, who represented earth and her fruitfulness. She came to me on a vision quest I did along the coast of Donegal in Ireland. Next was Sekhmet, an Egyptian warrior goddess connected to healing; she is portrayed as a lioness. Inanna is an ancient Sumerian goddess associated with love, sensuality, fertility, war and the planet Venus. Inanna is also connected with the lion. The fifth goddess is Quan Yin, a Chinese Buddhist goddess, who is the embodiment of compassionate loving kindness. The sixth goddess is the Nepalese Great Mother goddess Ghang Selmo.

Their instructions were quite specific. As their scribe I was to write a book about my experiences and my fellow eight mediums' experiences of talking to the dead during our monthly White Table sessions, including the teachings and guidance we received from the spirit world during the time of the Covid pandemic.

When we couldn't meet, we did our meditation session remotely from our own homes and then gathered on a Zoom call to share the messages we received. The teachings we received from the spirits included coping with fear, despair, all the grief, and getting nourishment from the trees and the beauty that surrounds us. One of their favorite suggested coping mechanisms was singing—a range of songs, including "Age of Aquarius" and the Beatles' "All You Need Is Love." Thankfully, the spirits weren't fussy about the quality of our voices. "Just sing or hum," they told us. Spirits and angels seem big on the healing nature of song.

Back to the writing of this book. So this is the deal. As I mentioned I am an artist, a master teacher, a shamanic practitioner, a person who likes her chocolate bars milk chocolate, not 92% dark. Writing is not my forte, and even my texts are challenging to read more like an e.e cummings poem,no caps or punctuation.

When the spirits told me that I was their scribe, then told me to write this book about my experiences with the dead and the White Table teachings from the spirits, I said "really? Not again!" Full disclosure: The spirits asked me to write a book four years ago called *Stalking the Sacred*, which was mostly about my spirit guides. (The curious reader can purchase it on Amazon.) I thought

I had completed, honorably I might add, my spiritual obligations regarding writing. But one does not refuse the requests from the spirit world.

Now I was forced to put into words what I often found difficult to describe. Words seem to make these ecstatic experiences small. Not to mention that these were rather personal experiences. I enjoy telling a good story but maybe these stories were a bit much. Right off the bat when I dutifully sat down to write this book, I was overcome with self-doubt: Who am I to write about the wisdoms coming from the spirit world? I am not a Jane Roberts *Seth Speaks* or a channel for a book like *A Course in Miracles.* (I even have a tough time believing in miracles, but I am working on it—the believing part.) Yes, I talk to the dead sometimes. Actually I prefer chatting with the dead to talking with most living people. Okay, that's a bit of an exaggeration. Let's just say I prefer to talk to the dead more than to strangers at a cocktail party.

To write about talking to the dead—it seemed a tall order, maybe even impossible for me. But I was a medium, I talk to my assorted spirit guides on a regular basis, so naturally I asked for healing and guidance from the spirit world. Tentatively, I began to slog through my mountain of resistance

14 Writing myself out of my writing block. I realized my fears of speaking my truth was the block.

Back to my process of writing this book. Through doing White Table remotely during the Covid lockdown, we received more guidance on dealing with what was happening in the world with Covid and firestorms and tragedies worldwide. That's where I started getting a little stuck in moving forward with writing. I got into my "I'm not worthy to write about this." I realized I was stuck—I had to get through my reluctance because the spirits told me that I was the scribe. They charged me with initially writing a book introducing White Table and talking to the dead.

So one way I connect with the spirits is by dialogue writing—writing out my conversations with them. I guess in some ways, I was trying to talk them out of having me as a scribe. Well, good luck with that

Then I went deeper to see what was stopping me, and that exploration was through a series of journeys and dances in an ancestor workshop with Sylvie Minot a Certified 5 Rhythms Teacher, executive director and founder of Syzygy Dance Project and is the creator of Medicine Circle. After these healing journeys I rewrote them as a myth. I realized that our journeys in Sylvie's class to non-ordinary reality are often stories of challenges and overcoming adversity with bravery.

After overcoming my challenges through these dance journeys, I could continue writing. Now the book was becoming richer because I'd added my own issues about speaking out as a woman, which I think is not only my issue but something many women face in daily life.

Superangel

15 Kvetching to the spirit: *A dialogue*

I decided I needed to enroll my spirit guides for guidance in writing this book. I also needed to whine a bit. One way I communicate with my guides is through dialogue writing. Here is where I started:

Pat: You told me that I am your scribe. Yes, I'll do it but you could have picked a real writer. I'm just saying. Okay, I tried to figure this book out in my head intellectually, and I have a bunch of index cards with chapter ideas. But you told me that this book is coming from the sacred realm and that I needed to stop trying to figure it out with my head. So here is my attempt to be more intuitive by dialoguing with you.

That's even a stretch for me. Yes, I know I've been studying shamanism and journeying for 30+ years. Okay, yes, when I make my art I get into a zone and the images come through me—marks, lines, colors, shapes. Art is my domain and practice, and I have some confidence in doing it for so many years.

No use arguing with you all as you gave me this job and I will do it. No more nattering. Let's start.

Okay, I'm saying a lot to calm myself; it's like humming. I have some questions for you.

What's the intention of this book?

Spirits: The book intends to relieve suffering and pain.

Pat: That's what I thought, especially around grief, loss of a loved one and the fear of death and dying. Then there is the question of what happens next after you die.

You spirits have given us a lot of teachings, especially during the past year, 2020, of the pandemic. This is the deal—I feel a bit odd, hesitant to share what you told us during our monthly White Table sessions. Yeah, self-doubt. Like, who am I to be the voice of the spirits?

And then I got their answer: Okay, I'm the voice for the spirits. These teachings need to be shared, and I can just park my ego under a tree and continue.

16 So now, instead of talking to the dead, we are talking to the spirits: *A dialogue*

Pat: I am a bit confused with the evolution of White Table. At first, we gathered around the White Table— white meaning that a white tablecloth covered the long table that we sat around. We were all dressed in white skirts and blouses as a way tomake it easier for the spirits to come through, less distractions.

We'd go into a trance after saying prayers of protection. We became mediums for souls who wanted help crossing over to the Light. Many times, the spirits who appeared were unknown to us. Occasionally, they were the famous deceased, like Leonard Cohen, Spinoza, or Joan of Arc. Most often, the spirits that came through were our own dead, like my husband, Charles; Erica's mother; Carol's horse; Sophia's grandmother; Ellen's aunt.

But yes, when the Covid pandemic hit, we had to stay at home and be isolated. So we had to do White Table remotely. Our work shifted. Even when we were still meeting in person, we'd begun getting more messages from the angels and spirits about more general things—fear, political despair, how to live in harmony with the environment. When we began meeting on Zoom, these messages became even more pronounced while the deceased souls needing help getting to the Light were fewer.This is still part of my questioning of the how White Table changed—from being mediums for deceased souls to being mediums for messages from the spirit world.

During Covid, at 4 p.m. on the first Sunday of the month, each of us, in our own house, would connect remotely to the others in our circle through meditation. This is when each of us got information—on how to be, on what was important; on how to keep our hearts open, deal with fear, and all the losses we were experiencing during this pandemic. For me when I sat down at my dining room table, I began to get information from the spirits, a download. After writing steadily for 30 minutes I was done, and it felt like I had become a writing medium for the spirits.

In the months that followed, very few individual souls appeared to us, asking for help. Instead, the souls streamed by on long boats or walking along a winding path up to the Light. These souls included the more than 6 million peoplethatwho have died worldwide so far from the Covid outbreak.

Here is an example of what I received in one White Table session done remotely in my own home during the Covid lockdown. I first smudged myself and called in all my power animals, teacher, and the Archangels.Then, at the designated time, I sat down, dressed in my white blouse and skirt, and mentally connected to the circle of my fellow mediums. I felt a circuit of energy and love connecting me to them.

White Table [virtual] 05.3.2020 Notes by Pat

I was reminded to fly above, and I changed into a hawk and flew above the earth. Time to visualize a different map, not the Covid map of the world but maps of the oceans, lakes, river, mountains—clear air, greenery, animals wandering in their natural habitats, watching the earth blooming with life and the beauty of all living beings.

Now is the time to go even deeper and deepen our connections to the natural world. These trees are our sisters and brothers—they are family, as are all living beings. The acknowledgement of these connections will support you, all of you, through these times.

Be LIGHT in weight and radiate light. Connect to the earth and also float above. You have been born to all the elements: earth, water, air, fire. Balance these within yourself.

REMEMBER who you really are, your true loving nature.

This is the time of GREAT LOVE. Love is what is to be spread throughout the world. Smell this sweetness, breathe in this love and then exhale it into the world. It will go where it is needed.

The spirits told us to do tonglen, which is Buddhist meditation practice designed to ease the suffering of others. You breathe the suffering in, you envision it being transformed inside you into love, and then it's love that you breathe out.

Breathe in the suffering, sadness and grief and breathe it out in an exhale. You are to bear witness but not take it in and internalize it, as that won't help. You all have been in training for this moment in time and you are not alone. You are part of this circle of light. You are surrounded by your angels, ancestors, teachers, helping spirits. Feel their love and energy.

Acts of IMAGINATION are important now.

The whole world needs to stop—the business, the destruction of the lands, the greed, the egos. This feeling of not belonging, nothing is enough, all this negativity has to stop.

This is the time for transformation and massive readjustment—a return to love, loving ourselves, others and all sentient beings. STILLNESS.

There is a reordering. We all have our memories—we don't need stuff to remind us. It is all inside us. Memories of a touch, a hug, the sound of a friend's laughter. This is a rich landscape that lives inside us.

Pat: "Is there something we need to know/understand to navigate these pandemic times?"

You are doing it.

Keep up your practices, whatever they may be.

Drink in nature.

Be full of thanks and gratitude.

LOVE is what connects us all to our true selves and each other.

Continue to be careful as you are living in the physical world.

Call on us for protection and do your own part. Be conscious.

You are needed now so BE PRESENT.

The Spirits asked me to please play the music (turn on the White Table play list).

It's a lullaby, these songs are soothing to us as there is much chaos, fear, anxiety about the spread of the virus—much grief.

I ask: How does the music soothe you?

It's the beauty, the melodies, the intention when it was created. These are sounds of hope and love. Music can open your hearts and chase away fear, dissolve anger.

Practice humming.

Sing to the stars, moon, and trees and return the bird's songs. And you never can get too much of Gregorian chant.

Let the music travel through your body into your bones, organs, and blood. Send the chants to those on your healing lists.

Keep telling your stories of your contact with the dead. Soon you will write again. They are teachings and need to be heard now—so much suffering, confusion and fear.

Stories are like Bach Fugues or a Van Gogh landscape. Listen, they reset your brain.

You tell your stories then your listener has permission to tell their stories.

This is how healing occurred in indigenous cultures. You come from a long line of storytellers.

Angel Celebrating Mother Earth

17 So many questions for you guys. *Another dialogue*

Pat: When we started White Table, it was all about helping souls cross over to the Light. We acted as the mediums for these souls, sometimes bringing messages from them to their loved ones who were here on earth. Then things shifted to this, receiving essential and valuable information from the spirits.

The next question is, "Are we still mediums? Are we now your messengers?" I like the idea of being a messenger for the spirit world. In Nara, Japan, the deer live freely in the parks as they are considered the messengers of the gods.

Spirits: You're our mediums. We liked how you were as mediums for the dead with so much love and respect that we chose you all to be our mediums.

Pat: You guys were a tad sneaky. I mean no disrespect but did you or do you ask us?

Spirits: It's part of the deal. When you step forward into doing work in the spirit world, you all declared yourself to do this work, and we accepted your offer. Now we, of course, have your back, flood you with light in love and healing. Not everyone can do this work, but you all together can and have and continue to do the work.

Pat: Yikes, that's really big. Maybe I should be more focused and take better care of my human body, like eating less sugar and flossing more. I'm not being flippant; I think my aging body reminds me of my old 2004 Highlander car—200,000 miles, struts sagging, paint peeling, though I know there isn't really a sense of time in the spirit world. Now what?

Spirits: This is where you, as our scribe, come in. You have been organizing and keeping the White table going consistently for over six years, gathering everyone's notes on what is coming through.

Pat: This is the part where I am a bit flummoxed. How do I or where do I begin?

Spirits: Again, you are not alone. We are here to help you and your White Table sisters.

18 Next, how exactly am I to write this book intuitively? *A dialogue*

Spirits: Just as you have set up this White Table with candles, Agua Florida, angel statues, golden egg rattles, Brigid's cloth, and playing sacred music, this is how you write this book:

Call the spirits of the six directions.

Sing your power song.

Sit down and meditate.

Then write.

You are writing our words, not your words. You are the vessel. Yes, we chose you as our scribe because of all the healing work you've done to be an empty bone to do your shamanic healing work. These writings are no different than when you prepare for shamanic healing; you fill yourself with power, and then you get out of the way, easy peasy. Do you have questions for us?

Pat: Do I need to write every day?

Spirits: Write when you can. It's vital to nourish yourself with visits with your friends and family.

Pat: No need for an outline, I guess.

Spirits: Remember you are an empty bone, as our scribe. You don't have an outline when you do shamanic healings, do you?

Pat: When I do a shamanic healing, I have no outline or plan. I just call on my spirit guides and follow where they lead me.I guess it's not a coincidence that last week you sent me three shamanic healings to do as well. Teach by doing?

Spirits: Yep.

Pat: Thank you. Sorry I'm so thick sometimes.

Spirits: Not thick just reluctant. Yes, we are pushing you a bit past your comfort zone.

Pat: I don't believe I have any more comfort zone left.

Spirits: You're a human being, right?

Pat: Yes, very human. Even though I unclutter my house, getting rid of furniture makes me sad—pieces left over from my failed second marriage.

Spirits: It wasn't a failure. More, your second marriage was a rite of passage.

Pat: I'd rather stick to four-day vision quests as my rites of passage. Oh yeah, I don't get to choose.

Spirits: Becoming a widow, getting divorced, and vision quests are all initiations to the spirit world.

Pat: I am full of gratitude. Okay, going back to the uncluttering. I feel my mind is getting uncluttered and it's okay to focus on one thing, like writing this book.

Spirits: Writing this book can be fun.

Pat: I have a bit of imposter syndrome going on. I just heard that term couple of weeks ago.

Spirits: Balderdash—an old story. Your new story is: I am a writer for the divine.

Pat: Sounds a bit pompous, don't you think?

Spirits: You are not pompous. There is power in speaking one's truth.

Pat: Maybe the more I speak the truth, the easier it will be to believe it as my truth.

Spirits: Not easier, just a way of being.

Pat: I like that "way of being."

Kickass Samurai Angel

19 Got an idea for the title yet? Just curious, don't mean to be pushy. *A dialogue*

Pat: What would you like me to call you spirits who come through the White Table and give us all these teachings and information? Y'all have a name?

Spirits: Right now, spirits will do. When it's the right time, we will reveal our names to you.

Pat: Okey dokey, next question. I seem to have quite a few questions. Do you guys have a name for this book? Initially, I thought it was Talking to the Dead, the Really Dead, and the Really Really Dead, but now I realize that it's much more than talking to the dead, so I need a better title. Travels Through the Veils? Actually, it's your book, so what do you like for the title? Or is it my job as your scribe to develop a title? Hmm, I am getting used to this idea of "as your scribe."

Spirits: The title will be revealed the more you write, so not to worry.

Pat: Just to recap, you guys don't have a name yet. We don't have a name for the book yet. I am not the book's author but rather your scribe.

Yes, I am embracing my walking between the two worlds. So, I guess I am a messenger for the spirit world. Man, I am a little slow to get this, but I got it now.

When I was thinking, as opposed to channeling, I saw that writing this book validated the existence of non-ordinary reality, and the experience of connecting with our deceased is a normal part of the grieving process. Hence, the White Table normalizes all this. The other part is that it helps people deal with their fear of death and what happens after they die. And now maybe it also opens people to the idea of letting the spirits guide us?

Spirits: This is the deal, as you would say. You just need to keep writing and keep writing and keep writing, and whenever you stop, that's not good because you slip into your judgmental mind. Just keep writing and trust this process. When you're doing a soul retrieval, you don't stop in the middle of the soul retrieval and ask the roadrunner where he's going or suggest you should go over there and not over there. He just flies in non-ordinary reality like a bat out of hell and you follow him, negotiating with him and the lost soul part. You need to be in that non-ordinary sacred space, and we can help you with that.

20 "All you need is love" *A dialogue*

Pat: Okay, how about The Good News About Being Dead as a title? I like it because it's kind of funny, especially since being dead freaks out a lot of people.

Spirits: Hmmm, not bad. We will work with you to set the tone for this book. Yes, folks are so afraid of being dead. Tell us more about the good news aspects of being dead.

Pat: Well first off, whenever we were doing White Table and being mediums for the departed souls, i.e. the dead, everyone was greeted with love. Walking through the veils and into the Light seemed like walking into a field of love.

Secondly, the information you all gave us during Covid in 2020 were messages of love. Reminding us that we are surrounded by love and that you always fill us with love and light. You also have been reminding us that love is the opposite of fear.

I just re-watched the movie *Michael* with John Travolta. Somewhere in our notes from White Table you suggested looking at that movie. The Archangel Michael, played by John Travolta, said that you've got to learn to laugh, and it's the way to true love. Then he got everyone driving in the car with him to sing the Beatles' "All You Need Is Love."

Spirits: When we say all you need is love, we mean all expressions of love: for your child, partner, best friend, dog, your garden, trees, something delicious, butterflies, and oh, yourself.

Pat: Yes, this business of loving ourselves is a tricky business, rather challenging actually.

Spirits: Necessary and vital to love oneself. Actually, love starts with oneself. As you say, "an inside job." Your core of self-love emanates outside you to others, to all beings. This is one of the reasons that when you do White Table, we surround you with love. It permeates your beings. It is the energy source and why you can contact the dead and help them crossover.

Pat: When we do White Table, we often report that we see angels, see their wings, and feel their presence. Angels are kind of new for me in the spirit world. The nuns in my Catholic catechism class were more into the nuances of mortal sin and the joys of purgatory. Not much mention of angels, but Michael, Raphael, Gabriel, Uriel, and Metatron became our protectors in White Table. We would call them in at the beginning of each session to create a dome of protection over us. I know people are drawn to angels or feel angels are accessible spirits. Why is that?

Spirits: Angels are included and described in many religions, including Christianity, Judaism, and Islam. These angels are often depicted as humans with wings, making them very relatable.

Pat: One time at White table, I was the medium for the Angel of Death. Instead of being a scary grim reaper sporting a scythe, this angel was more like a fat Renaissance cherub who madly whistled. Partly to annoy, partly to bring humor to this whole business of death, his message was that death is not to be feared. We were all so charmed by him and by the idea that that's who will come for you when you die. We started to refer to him as the Whistling Cherub of Death.

Angel Gathers Flowers of Hope

21 Sometimes, I would have private angel conversations

For example, during one Zoom White Table I was told to keep doing standup comedy about the afterlife. The spirits told me, you can teach through comedy and you're good at it.

Also, they suggested that I begin to trust Parker, my golden doodle teenager, that I was to practice speaking to him through mental telepathy. He is psychic too.

About the book:

You are dancing through your resistances, and they are as strong as you think. Dance is another way we can support you.

Notice the people who are showing up in your life to support you.

You are not alone. Notice the books you are drawn to read.

Trust your intuition when it tells you to call a friend

Yes, at this point in your life you need a lot of solitude. Trust this.

Yes, love will blossom in your life—bringing in much change, new energies.

Meanwhile, keep doing your work: Write, draw and be present.

Keep asking your dad to be your guide and to journey with you

Keep trusting your writing process. The book is as much about this process as our teachings and helping souls cross over.

22 Angels are the gateway to the spirit world

The thing is, it's easy to talk to angels. You just have to want talk to them. It's simple; just start chatting the angels up like you would a dear friend. Okay, so it takes a bit of imagination and maybe a little leap of faith. But they're very accessible. That's why angels have been part of cultural traditions throughout time and the world. One of the things I realized in my contact with the Archangels is that they want to help us. For the angels to help us, we ask them directly. Angels are not mind readers, and that can't just barge into our lives without being invited. Asking for help is a significant tenet of communicating with all spirits, Angels, power animals, and our ancestors.

Angels also communicate with symbols. Several weeks ago, I noticed the tire pressure warning light on my red Kia Soul. I checked the pressure, kicked the tires and gave each tire some air. My warning sign went on for three days until I looked at the tread on my front tires, discovering they were bald as billiard balls. I high-tailed it to the tire store and gleefully brought four new tires. Later that week, I drove up to the White Mountains with my new full-of-tread tires hugging the road. On my way home, I stopped at the bottom of the Salt River Canyon to let my Doodle, Parker, sniff around. I looked at the SUV next to me and saw a 3-foot image of angel wings decal on their car's rear window.I felt like the angels just winked at me by showing me those angel wings. "Yikes," I said. "First, the angels gave me a warning light about my tires. Luckily, I paid attention and bought those new tires."

The other thing I noticed about having Archangels as part of my life is that I no longer feel alone. I mean, it's not like I sit at my house at my dining room table chatting to the invisible Spirits. (Actually, sometimes I do.) But I have a sense that they're with me. I often ask the Archangels to protect me when I'm driving.

Several years ago (pre-Covid) I traveled back to Ireland to visit some of my favorite sacred sites including the Paps of Anu, the Seven Sister stone circle, and Brigid's Well in Kildare.I decide to rent a tiny stick shift car in Killarney. Driving on the left side of the road is a challenge, shifting gears is a challenge as I often find myself turning on the turn signals instead of shifting the gear. The biggest challenge though was entering roundabouts that were ass-backwards from what I was used to.I decided I needed some spiritual protection beyond my power animals. Having invited the Archangels for a visit several times, I decided to ask them to join me as Idrove along the Wild Atlantic coast of western Ireland.After I completed the car rental paperwork, I asked the angels to jump aboard.

Right off the get-go as I stalled at the first round about, I felt their patient support, and with each roundabout I avoided getting broadsided and gained more confidence. One day up in the Burren we spent a day driving around, looking for St. Colman's well. Maybe Archangels aren't perfect at following maps but because I felt their presence, it felt like an adventure.

The next day, after asking my Irish friend about the location of the well, we found it. There wasn't exactly a big sign indicating its location, but it turned out to be a truly magical spot complete with a tree to tie ribbons for blessings next to the holy well.

Sometimes I ask the Archangels to come into my dreams and to help me solve problems. They are my partners in writing this book. When I get stuck, I either dialogue with the angels or journey to them, asking for their guidance.

When I want to communicate with the angels, it helps to create a calm space, maybe light a candle, sit still for a minute, close my eyes and focus on my question.

Friendship with angels is available to everyone. What I appreciate about communicating with the angels is that it is simple and straightforward, no intermediary needed, nor having a particular belief.

Angel Offering Bouquets of Love

23 Talking to our dead, power animals and assorted helping spirits, angel included

I am interested in what happens when we die and whether it is possible to communicate with our deceased loved ones. This quest led me to communicate with power animals, spirit guides, and eventually my deceased ancestors through shamanic drumming. In these trance states of non-ordinary reality, I experienced the river of light and love that greets our loved ones when they die.

I am relieved that my dad and mom and husband Charles and my sister Pam are in a safe, healing place full of love. This awareness makes me no longer fear death. After we leave our bodies and this earth plane, we're on our next adventure. The ancient Celts call this place Tir na og. I find all this reassuring and reinforced by what my deceased loved ones have told me during the White Table ceremonies.

When I discovered shamanism, an ancient spiritual practice practiced for 100,000 years, I was intrigued when I realized that by listening to a recording of a repetitious drumbeat or even rattling a box of Tic Tacs, I could have direct contact with the spirit world. I could also tap into the ancestors' wisdom and experience about how all life is alive and connected. The shamanic journey has become my practice over the past forty years.

Once I realized I could communicate with the dead, a new world opened. Though getting there was painful.It took the sudden death of my best friend, art partner, and husband, Charles, and sinking into grief. I wasn't ready to totally lose Charles, and I wanted to find a new way to have a relationship with him. There are many ways to create relationships with our deceased loved ones; the trick is to be open and receptive.

I remember a dream I had about four months after Charles died. In the dream, I went out to get into my 1974 yellow Chevy Nova, only to find my front right tire was completely flat. Charles appeared and offered to change it for me. As much as I hate changing tires, I told him no; I knew he was dead and said I needed to learn how to do these things myself.

Whenever I see a hawk flying above me on my walks in the desert, I know it's Charles checking in. When we used to take walks in the desert Charles always noticed the hawks flying overhead and would point them out to me. The first year after I finally connected with my dad in the spirit world, I put his number in my phone. Of course, I mean a made-up number, but I found it comforting to see his name on my phone. Although these are small acts, they helped me through my grief. An unexpected gift of White Table has been a new connection with the angels.

Angel of the Goldfishes

24 You too can contact your dead

There are a lot of resources on how to help folks connect with their dead, including psychics, mediums, teachers of shamanic journeying, spiritual directors, and mentors. As a note of caution, you want to vet these people first. Also, I am not suggesting that everyone set up their White Table sessions, as training is essential.

If you find yourself stuck in grief, trying one or more of these things might be worthwhile. Connecting with the angels is available to everyone, regardless of their belief system. It is fun and easy and is a beautiful antidote to feeling alone and unsupported. See the instructions for Inviting the Five Archangels into Your Home.

Here are a few simple suggestions for connecting with your dead:

- See a psychic or medium.
- Learn shamanic journeying yourself.

- Ask your deceased loved one to come into your dream time.
- Notice something in the natural world that makes you think of them, like a butterfly or the color pink or a Ford Mustang.
- Write them a letter.
- Tell stories about them; it's a way to keep their memories alive.
- During the Days of the Dead, October 31st-November 1st, make an altar, put up their photographs, favorite food, and drink.
- Go out to your favorite place in nature and sit; be still and listen.
- Make a simple homemade book or buy a notebook and fill it full of your stories about them—the good, the bad, the ugly, and the beautiful. They were human once too, and you're human now.

Eighty percent of people experience contact with their dead in the first year following the death of someone close to them. These experiences are essential and must be validated and shared with people who understand. Otherwise, those who experience this contact are left feeling marginalized or discredited.

If people have the experience of contacting their dearly departed or think it might be possible to speak to their dead, this could be very healing. Also, if people had a sense that there was another reality where they could connect to their loved ones, it would bring home the possibility that our loved ones have not entirely gone into the cosmos, never to be heard or seen again.

25 The angels made me do it

These angels pushed themselves into my life, rearranging some priorities and hijacking my art. I'm not complaining. Let's back up a bit. My first experience with angels was seeing paintings of angels in my Renaissance art history classes in college. I loved Giotto's small angelic spirits hovering over the scenes of Crucifixion in Arena Chapel, Padua. Later, when I lived in Florence, I occasionally popped into the Convent of San Marco to look at the Archangel Gabriel visiting the Virgin Mary in The Annunciation fresco by Fra Angelico. What I noticed about these angels was their solemness.They had a job to do, whether it was protection, witnessing, or delivering messages. Later, when I looked at images of guardian angels from the last 100 years, these angels seemed saccharine without the seriousness of purpose.

When I started to paint angels, mine were a wild, goofy bunch, full of vibrant colors and often humorous. My style became more playful and sometimes irreverent. I began to paint the angels I was calling on—or wishing would appear. When I was painting an angel with enormous blue wings, I put Superman's S on his chest, and he then became the *Super Angel Who Helps You When You Are Stuck*. I painted a beautiful angel based on the Statue of Liberty to make a statement about welcoming immigrants, just as was the case with my great grandfather fleeing from the famine in Ireland. .

I found the way these angels have become an influential part of my life both amusing and surprising. They have unexpectedly helped me financially, as people

enjoy buying angel notecards or giclee prints of my angels. Also, they tell me not to worry about money as they have my back, although spirits are a little vague regarding numbers. Now I have expanded my creative expression beyond art and writing to include performance pieces of stand-up angel story telling. These guys seem to be enjoying being seen in this new accessible and fun way.

My relationships with the angels have given me comfort about dying, although I must chat them up about getting to dead when I have moments of the heebie jeebies. I used to be reluctant to speak about my connections to the spirit world but now it's easy. Talking to my angels and asking for guidance feels like chatting with dear friends. Also they are showing up more and more in White Table, giving us information on coping with these challenging times and surrounding us in light and love. I am also much more aware of miracles in my life: my new granddaughter, two knees full of metal that make walking fun, my oak trees surviving the Arizona drought, and finding a dancing partner in a 60-pound golden doodle.

My catechism nuns used to talk about sanctifying grace and how sin puts a kibosh on all that grace. In White Table, we experience no blame with the dead, just unconditional love. Angels are full of Light and love and are playful with a marvelous sense of humor.They are that sanctifying grace, eternal and omnipresent. The good news is we cannot put a kibosh on them.But we can invite them into our lives.

I hope that after reading this book, you are open to the possibility that there is a spiritual realm with spirits ready to heal and guide you. A place to begin could be to host the Archangels in your home for five days. Who knows what you might discover?

Many Blessings

Ancient Angel

Hosting the Archangels for five days in your home

In 2010, Irmi, a German medium, experienced a visit by some unnamed chosen angels, highly placed in the angel hierarchy. They asked her to share her experiences of their visit so that others might invite them into their lives.

It requires some preparation, though the prep is simple and easy to follow. The Archangels stay with you for five days, bringing healing, support, and much more to assist you and your journey. Here is the information that will prepare and help you host the five Archangels.

PREPARATION

You will welcome and host the Archangels for five days after preparing an altar.

Include the following items for your altar.

1. A single white flower or a bouquet of white flowers

2. A candle that will stay on all the time they are with you. It needs to be lit shortly before the Archangels arrive to show them they are welcome in your home. Nowadays, you can also find battery-lit "candles."

3. Write a letter to angels with three wishes: one for Mother Earth, one for your family, one for you.Formulate the wishes clearly and concisely. Not too

much detail. Then seal the letter in an envelope.

4. Set an apple (that you will eat after they leave) on top of the sealed envelope and lay the envelope near your candle and white flower. If an apple doesn't work, choose a yummy food item.

5. The house must be clean and tidy, much like you would tidy it if you received a guest.

WELCOMING THE 5 ARCHANGELS

Welcome the five Archangels. When they arrive at 10:30 p.m. (or earlier if that is too late for you), open the front door and read this greeting out loud:

"Hello and welcome Archangels to my home. I am very grateful to you for you coming for a visit and bringing peace to my home and to beings who live here. Thank you for bringing your gifts of harmony, joy, and serenity."You can also say a greeting in your own words. Remember: angels aren't sticklers for the rules.

From that moment on, the Archangels make things happen. Regard the five days as a particular time to find room for the vibration of higher energies to re-align many things.

DURING THEIR VISIT

You want to ask questions or find a quiet moment to meditate with each of them in your busy day. But remember, there is no limitation. TRUST!!! You can also ask them to go with you through the day.

Remember that by hosting the five Archangels—Michael, Gabriel, Raphael, Uriel, and Metatron—you are assisting them to serve humanity and Mother Earth. They thank you for your willingness to participate.

ON THE LAST DAY

When it's almost time for them to leave (before 10:30 p.m.), express your gratitude to the Archangels for all they have brought you. Give more thanks and good wishes as they journey on to spread their hope, light, and love to others. When you send them on, say:

"Thank you for visiting me and my home and bringing harmony, joy, and serenity to all of us. Thank you for all your blessings and healings and for answering my prayers. I am sending you my love to accompany you all on your travels." Or say the prayer that feels right to your own heart.

ONCE THEY LEAVE

Burn the envelope with your wishes, which frees up the energy and manifests the wishes. Take the ashes and put them out into the wind.

Express your gratitude. Eat your apple (or other food); it will contain lots of good nutrients and more. Place the flower outside directly on Mother Earth so that it recycles naturally.

Enjoy your special time with the angels! You can always host them again yourself. You do NOT need to be home the whole time the angels are with you, though you do need to welcome them at 10:30 pm when they arrive and see them out five nights later. You can bring the angels with you to work, and they don't have to "leave" necessarily. They can be in multiple places at once, but you will have a unique experience of connecting with them during these five days when you honor them. Enjoy your experience with your visit with these remarkable angels!

The Five Archangels

The Five Archangels are: Michael, Gabriel, Raphael, Uriel, and Metatron. It's fun to learn more about them. Here is a place to start:

Archangel Michael: Head Archangel. His name means "One who looks like God." Michael clears toxins associated with fear and assists in people's life purpose and career path. The angel of abundance, protection, defense, power, justice, and strength.

Archangel Gabriel: Brings good news in abundance, discerning messages received and what we give out. Messenger between Heaven and Earth. The angel of communication, writing and art. Balancer of energies.

Archangel Raphael: Healer of mind, thoughts, body and soul, custodian of The Tree of Life (Kabbalah). God's Physician.

Archangel Uriel: Angel of enlightenment, unconditional forgiveness, heals every aspect of your life. Peace.

Archangel Metatron: Angel who looks after children, led the children of Israel out of the wilderness. Can transmute time and space as well as a master of Sacred Geometry.

GLOSSARY

Mediumship A medium is someone who can communicate with deceased souls who are on the other side. Mediums can act as vessels for spirits needing a human form to communicate with this world. There are several different ways mediums receive their information from the spirits:

Clairvoyance or clear seeing is the ability to see anything that is physical but not present. Often the medium can see the (deceased) person and even describe what they're wearing.

Clairaudience clear hearing. The ability to hear voices of the spirits. Sometimes the medium experiences a soul as if standing beside them and speaking to them in conversation.

Clairsentience or clear feeling is a condition in which the medium takes on the ailments of the spirit, feeling the same physical problems that the spirit had experienced before their death.

Medium experiences may involve multiple senses: seeing the spirit in the mind's eye, mentally hearing, and sometimes feeling sensations in the body.

Spiritism first developed in Brazil during the second half of the 19th century as a mediumship religion identifying with French educator Allan Kardec. Kardec defined Spiritism as a philosophy, a religion, and a science.

Séance is a meeting at which people attempt to make contact with the dead, primarily through the agency of a medium.

Spiritism and White Table

White Table comes out of the tradition of Spiritism, as practiced by the Sauer family from Brazil. Whereas Spiritism often uses séances, White Table gave these séances a specific form, beginning with the fact that the participants wear white and gather around a table covered in white. The mediums also place their hands on the table creating a circuit of energy.

Brazilian Pass is an aura cleansing technique used to purify the mediums before White Table ceremonies.

Shamanism is a practice that involves a practitioner (**shaman**) interacting with what they believe to be a *spirit world* through *altered states of consciousness*, such as *trance*. This goal is usually to direct *spirits* or *spiritual energies* into the physical world for healing, *divination*, or to aid human beings in some other way.

Shamanic Journeying

Shamanic journeying and non-ordinary reality are terms coined and popularized by Michael Harner, author of *The Way of the Shaman*. Shamanic journeying is a technique used to enter into trance states. A shaman or shamanic practitioner plays a beat on a drum generally around 140–160 bpm. By listening to this repetitious pulse, they go into a trance state (the non-ordinary reality) in which they can communicate with totem animals, and spirit guides and encounter other entities to answer questions or retrieve objects in this spirit world.

Shamanic cosmology

In shamanic cosmology, non-ordinary reality is divided into the Upper-, Lower-, and Middle worlds. To access the wisdom and healing of these worlds, the shaman must enter non-ordinary reality or an altered state of consciousness. The shaman travels through these three worlds to gather information and medicines specific to the person they are working with.

Power animals

Power animals have been around for millennia and are a core component of shamanism. Shamans are people who work with the spirit world to help bring about healing at the spirit or soul level, which can also result in physical, mental or emotional healing as well. All shamans work with Power animals, but Power animals are not limited to just shamans. Power animals are available and want to work with everyone and can be invaluable guides in our lives.

A **psychopomp** is a person or being who conducts deceased souls to the otherworld. Classic examples of a psychopomp are the ancient Egyptian god Anubis, the Greek ferryman Charon, and the Norse Valkyries.

Deposession

A method of Shamanic healing that liberates a suffering deceased being who exists within the host person's energy field.

Ayahuasca is a brew made from the leaves of the Psychotria viridis shrub along with the stalks of the *Banisteriopsis caapi* vine. This drink was used for spiritual and religious purposes by ancient Amazonian tribes and is still used as a sacred beverage in ceremonies conducted by the shamans in the Amazonian rainforests.

Light, the capped version is used as a destination—going to the Light— but lower case is used for the more common noun: we send her love and light.

Tonglen is a Buddhist meditation practice designed to ease the suffering of others.

Tir na nog: In Irish mythology Tir na nog ("Land of the Young") is one of the names for the Celtic Otherworld.

Catechism

The *Baltimore Catechism No. 1* presents the Catholic faith basics in a manner suitable for first communicants through fifth graders.It was the national Catholic catechism for children in the United States, based on Robert Bellarmine's 1614 *Small Catechism*. The first such catechism written for

Catholics in North America was the standard Catholic school text in the country from 1885 to the late 1960s.

Purgatory

In Roman Catholic doctrine, Purgatory is a place or state of suffering inhabited by the souls of sinners atoning for their sins before going to heaven.mortal sin

In the moral theology of Catholicism, a mortal sin requires that all of the following conditions are met:

1. Its subject matter must be grave.
2. It must be committed with full knowledge (and awareness) of the sinful action and the gravity of the offense.
3. It must be committed with deliberate and complete consent.[9]

The seven deadly sins are the seven behaviors or feelings that inspire further sin. They are **pride**, **greed**, **lust**, **envy**, **gluttony**, **wrath**, and **sloth**.

RESOURCES

The Spirits' Book, Alan Kardec

The Way of the Shaman, Michael Harner

Stalking the Sacred, Pat Dolan

Talking to Heaven, James Van Praagh

Reunions, Raymond Moody

Shamanism, Sandra Ingerman

The Wild Edge of Sorrow, Frances Weller

Angels, an Endangered Species, Malcolm Godwin

The Glory of Angels, Edward Lucie-Smith

A Book of Angels, Sophy Burnham

Grief Counseling and Grief Therapy, J. William Worden

Workshops and Classes with Pat Dolan

- Discover how to conduct White Table Sessions,
- Explore communicating with angels and spirit animals, weekend individual retreats at Brigid's Well in Oracle, Arizona—a time to explore your creative self, including visual arts and writing.
- Engage in art classes in pastel, opaque watercolor, and Sumi ink with an emphasis on a sense of play and having fun.in person or Zoom
- Spiritual and creativity mentoring via Zoom

Angel art, prints, and angel cards can be viewed on Pat's website **www.patdolan.net**

Earth Angel

through stars, I fly
embracing leaps of faith
no longer silenced

—Pat Dolan

Made in the USA
Las Vegas, NV
03 December 2022

61040470R10083